Get Cooking with Mickey & Friends

Allergy-Friendly Fun for the Family

Sharing a delicious meal with family members is, perhaps, the most enjoyable part of each day! Research shows that the families who eat together also grow together.

However, for the food-allergic individual, eating any meal can be a stressful and challenging ordeal. By following these simple and fun-to-make recipes, you can create enticing, nutritious, and allergy-friendly meals for your whole family. Make meal planning and preparation a family event; cooking can be both fun and educational, not only for the food-allergic person but for other family members as well.

The recipes in this book are clearly labeled to indicate whether milk, eggs, fish, shellfish, tree nuts, peanuts, wheat, or soy are included, with substitution notes to help you avoid your family's particular allergens. You'll also find great tips on how to handle your allergies when eating out at restaurants, handling food at school and parties, and more! And remember, regardless of the dining setting, in a restaurant or at home, keep two epinephrine auto-injectors nearby—just in case an unexpected allergic reaction occurs.

So roll up your sleeves, put on your chef's apron, select your favorite dish, and let's have some FUN!

—*Dr. Dana Wallace, M.D., Associate Clinical Professor*
at Nova Southeastern University.

Dr. Wallace is with the Florida Center for Allergy & Asthma Care and the former President of the American College of Allergy, Asthma and Immunology (ACAAI). She has been practicing medicine for more than 20 years.

Note: Photographs may contain additional food items or a different serving size than reflected in the nutritional analysis.

Before You Get Started

Reading Food Labels

Did you know that eight foods contribute to the majority of food-related severe allergic reactions? They are **milk, eggs, fish, shellfish, tree nuts, peanuts, wheat, and soy.** The Food Allergen Labeling and Consumer Protection Act of 2004 (FALCPA) requires that all food labels containing these allergens must clearly identify the food allergens in one of two ways on the ingredient list. The allergen may either:

- **be identified by following the ingredient listing with the word "Contains" followed by the major food allergen (for example: "Contains milk, wheat, etc.")**

- **be listed in the ingredient list in parentheses (for example: "albumin (eggs)")**

These allergens must be listed if they are added in any amount in the food, even in artificial or natural flavors, spice blends, or coloring. Additionally, manufacturers must list the specific nut (i.e. walnut, cashew, etc.) and the specific crustacean shellfish (i.e. crab, shrimp, lobster, etc.) that is being used.

Some food packaging may have an advisory label which is shown as a "may contain" statement. "May contain" means that non-allergenic foods MAY come in contact with any of the eight major allergens. This is known as cross-contact. This label is voluntary for manufacturers. There are no laws mandating these statements, so they may not indicate if a product may

"May contain" phrases may appear in several ways. Foods may also say "processed in a facility that also processes" or "made on equipment with."

contain trace elements of a specific major food allergen.

If you are ever unsure whether or not a product may contain your allergen, it's best to call the manufacturer directly to ask about their ingredients and manufacturing processes.

Did you know that ingredients in food can change without warning? Be sure to read the labels on all food packages EVERY TIME you buy something.

Food Substitutions

Some of the recipes in this book may call for ingredients your child can't eat. Here are some substitutions you can make:

Top Dairy Substitutes:

- **Soy milk** can be substituted for dairy milk. You can also use rice, sunflower, hemp, or coconut milk if you have an allergy to soy. When substituting milk, use a one-to-one ratio. If a recipe calls for one cup of milk, one cup of *any* milk alternative will work. Note: goat's milk is NOT a safe substitute for dairy milk, as both contain similar proteins.

- **Dairy-free margarine and shortening** can easily be found at your local grocery store and make excellent substitutes for butter. Use 1 cup of margarine for every cup of butter being replaced.

- **Dairy-free sour cream, cream cheese**, and **other cheeses** can be found in your local grocery store. Be sure to read the labels carefully, especially when it comes to cheeses, as some "soy" cheeses contain milk.

Top Egg Substitutes:

- For baking, each egg can be replaced with **¼ cup unsweetened applesauce** or **¼ cup mashed banana**. A mixture of **1½ Tbsp. water, 1½ Tbsp. vegetable oil**, and **1 tsp. baking powder** can also be substituted for each egg. **Powdered egg substitute** is also available.

- To coat meats, replace each egg with **1 Tbsp. water** or **vegetable oil**.

- As a binding ingredient, replace each egg with **1 Tbsp. flax meal** and **3 Tbsp. hot water**; let stand 5 minutes until thickened. Each egg can also be replaced by **1 Tbsp. apricot puree.**

Top Nut Substitutes:

- Peanut butter can easily be replaced with **sunflower butter**, **soy butter** (if your child does not have a soy allergy), or **almond/cashew butter** (if your child does not have a tree nut allergy).

Soy Substitutes:

- **Coconut milk, coconut oil,** or **coconut yogurt** can be used as a substitute for recipes that call for soy (tofu, soy milk, some cream cheese).

- Other milks such as **rice, oat, hemp,** or **potato** can be used interchangeably with soy milk or dairy milk.

Wheat Substitutes:

- **All-purpose gluten-free flour blend** can be used as a substitute for regular all-purpose flour. Add **½ to 1 tsp. xanthan gum** per cup of gluten-free flour blend to act as a binding ingredient.

- A cup of breadcrumbs can be replaced by **¾ cup unsweetened rice flakes** or **1 cup oatmeal**.

- For baking, **1 cup wheat flour** may be replaced by **1 cup corn flour** or **⅞ cup white rice flour**.

Keep an eye out for the colored icons throughout the book. They will let you know about allergens for which you may need to make substitutions.

Hidden Ingredients:

These ingredients may include or be made from wheat:

- Bread crumbs
- Bulgur
- Cereal extract
- Club wheat
- Couscous
- Cracker meal
- Durum
- Einkorn
- Emmer
- Farina
- Flour
- Hydrolyzed wheat protein
- Kamut®
- Matzoh, matzoh meal (also spelled matzo, matzah, or matza)
- Pasta
- Seitan
- Semolina
- Spelt
- Sprouted wheat
- Triticale
- Vital wheat gluten
- Wheat bran hydrolysate
- Wheat germ oil
- Wheatgrass
- Wheat protein isolate
- Whole wheat berries

Did you know that ingredients can go by several names or may show up in unexpected places? For example, some marshmallows contain eggs. Here are a few key words to watch out for.

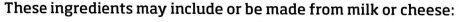

These ingredients may include or be made from milk or cheese:

- Butter or artificial butter flavor
- Casein
- Caseinates (ammonium, calcium, magnesium, and potassium)
- Curds
- Diacetyl
- Ghee
- High protein flour
- Hydrolysates (casein, milk protein, whey, and whey protein)
- Lactalbumin and lactalbumin phosphate
- Lactoferrin
- Lactoglobulin
- Lactose
- Malted, condensed, evaporated, dry, whole, low-fat, nonfat, skimmed, and goat milk
- Milk derivative, milk protein, and milk solids
- Nougat
- Pudding
- Recaldent™
- Rennet casein
- Some flavorings, such as caramel, cream, coconut cream, and chocolate
- Sour milk solids
- Tagatose
- Tuna fish (which may be made with casein
- Whey (delactosed, demineralized, and protein concentrate)
- Yogurt

These ingredients may include or be made from eggs:

- Albumin (also spelled albumen)
- (Egg) lecithin
- Egg substitutes (note: Egg Beaters® is not a safe alternative for eggs)
- Egg white, egg yolk, dried egg, and powdered egg
- Eggnog
- Globulin
- Livetin
- Lysozyme
- Mayonnaise
- Meringue
- Ovalbumin
- Ovomucin
- Ovomucoid
- Ovovitellin
- Surimi
- Vitellin

These ingredients may include or be made from soy:

- Edamame
- Miso
- Natoo
- Soya
- Soybean (curds, granules)
- Soy protein (concentrate, hydrolyzed, isolate)
- Shoyu
- Soy sauce
- Tamari
- Tempeh
- Textured Vegetable Protein (TVP)
- Tofu

These ingredients may include or be made from peanuts:

- Artificial nuts
- Cold-pressed, expeller pressed, or extruded peanut oil
- Ground nuts
- Mixed nuts
- Monkey nuts
- Nougat
- Nu-Nuts
- Nut pieces
- Nut meat
- Peanut butter
- Peanut flour
- Peanut protein hydrolysate

These ingredients may include or be made from fish:

- Barbecue sauce
- Bouillabaisse
- Caesar salad
- Caviar
- Deep-fried items
- Fish flavoring
- Fish flour
- Fish fumet
- Fish gelatin (kosher gelatin, marine gelatin)
- Fish oil
- Fish sauce (imitation fish or shellfish, isinglass lutefisk maw, fish maws, maws)
- Fish stock
- Fishmeal
- Nuoc mam (Vietnamese name for fish sauce)
- Roe
- Salad dressing
- Seafood flavoring
- Shark cartilage
- Shark fin
- Surimi
- Sushi, sashimi
- Worcestershire sauce

These ingredients may include shellfish:

- Barnacle
- Crab
- Crawfish (crawdad, crayfish, écrevisse)
- Krill
- Lobster (langouste, langoustine, Moreton Bay bugs, scampi, tomalley)
- Prawns
- Shrimp (crevette, scampi)

Lifestyle Tip: Cross-Contact and Effective Cleaning

Even if you aren't preparing food, don't forget to wash your hands before and after every meal!

If you have a food allergy or take care of someone with a food allergy, it is very important to avoid cross-contact between foods. Cross-contact occurs when one food comes into contact with another food and their proteins mix. As a result of the cross-contact, the two foods contain small amounts of each other. For example, if a knife has been used to spread peanut butter and is wiped off but not properly cleaned, the protein from the peanut butter can be transferred to the next food the knife is used on. The amount of protein is usually so small that it can't be seen, but to someone with food allergies, this cross-contact can cause a severe allergic reaction.

Eating at home:

Avoiding cross-contact begins at home with effective cleaning methods. All cooking surfaces, equipment, and utensils must be cleaned with hot, soapy water before being used to prepare allergen-free food. Studies have shown that bar and liquid soap are effective at removing food allergen protein from your hands; alcohol-based sanitizer is not considered an effective cleaner. Make sure to wash your hands thoroughly with warm, soapy water before you start cooking or serving food and to properly wash knives, spoons, and other cooking utensils between each use. For cleaning work surfaces, one tsp. of concentrated bleach per one gallon of water at normal room temperature works best. Be sure to allow the surface to air dry after sanitizing, as wiping with a cloth could introduce new allergens. If you wear gloves or an apron when cooking, make sure to change these before serving any food or before handling allergen-free food. You may want to consider having a dedicated washing bin and washcloth for cleaning the plateware and silverware of the person with food allergies.

Eating out:

Effective cleaning at home is important, but it is equally important to be aware of cross-contact when dining out at restaurants. For example, steak and hamburger rolls are often buttered for extra flavor, but butter is not listed as an ingredient on the menu. For someone with a dairy allergy, this cross-contact could lead to a severe reaction. Always be sure to tell your server about the severity of your food allergy, and talk to a manager or the chef about the procedures for preparing allergen-free meals. You may want to call the restaurant you wish to dine at beforehand to talk to the chef about your concerns. Chef cards are a great tool to use for communication between the wait staff and the cook. These cards list your dietary restrictions and emergency contact information. The chef and the manager want you to have a great dining experience, so be sure to discuss your allergy with them.

Breakfast

Mickey's Good Morning Granola

(Serves 6)

Calculated using ¼ cup raisins

Calories: 170   Total Fat: 3.5 grams   Total Carbohydrate: 30 grams   Fiber: 4 grams   Protein: 5 grams

Mickey knows there's nothing like a healthy breakfast of granola to get his morning started right.

Ingredients:

2 cups plain granola

¼ cup raw sunflower seeds

¼ cup dried fruits, such as chopped apricots, pineapple bits, cranberries, and/or raisins

Allergy note:

Many granolas have nuts in them. Be sure to read ingredients for your allergens, or use homemade granola.

Directions:

1. Stir the granola and sunflower seeds together in a big bowl.

2. Choose the dried fruit you want to add. You can pick one or mix a few together. Add the fruit to the bowl.

3. Stir the granola until all the ingredients are well mixed. It's ready to eat right away.

 TIP Granola is more than just a breakfast cereal. It also tastes great sprinkled on ice cream or even tossed in a salad.

Minnie's Homemade Jam

(Makes ½ cup)

Calories: 45   Total Fat: 0 grams   Total Carbohydrate: 11 grams   Fiber: 1 grams   Protein: 0 grams

Ingredients:

1 cup sliced strawberries

3 Tbsp. cold water

2 tsp. cornstarch

2 Tbsp. sugar

TIP Spice up your jam by making a jam and cream cheese sandwich! Or if you have a milk allergy, try pairing it with sunflower butter!

Minnie loves spending time in nature, especially when she goes berry picking. After all, fresh berries make the best jam!

Directions:

1. Put the strawberries in a medium-size heavy saucepan. Use a potato masher or fork to crush them up.

2. In a small bowl, mix the cold water and cornstarch together. Then mix in the sugar.

3. Combine the cornstarch mixture with the strawberries in the saucepan. Heat the strawberry mixture on medium-low until the mixture starts to bubble. Then turn the heat down to low and cook for 4 to 5 minutes, stirring all the while.

4. Remove the pan from the heat and set aside until the jam cools.

Donald's Sticky Bread

(Serves 10)

Calories: 370   Total Fat: 13 grams   Total Carbohydrate: 60 grams   Fiber: 0 grams   Protein: 4 grams

Ingredients:

3 cups wheat-free flour

4 tsp. baking powder

1 tsp. salt

⅓ cup cold butter

1¼ cup milk

½ cup brown sugar

½ cup white sugar

1 tsp. cinnamon

6 Tbsp. butter, melted

Allergy Substitution Note:

In case of milk allergy, use a milk alternative and dairy-free margarine.

Sometimes it takes a little convincing to get Donald to share his bread. With this sweet and sticky pull-apart treat, there's plenty for everybody!

Directions:

1. Heat the oven to 375°F. Generously grease a nonstick fluted tube pan.

2. In a mixing bowl, stir together the flour, baking powder, and salt. With a table knife, cut the butter into small pieces. Use your fingertips to pinch the butter into the flour mixture until the lumps of butter are about the size of peas. Then stir in the milk.

3. Turn the dough onto a floured surface and knead it for about 5 seconds. Pull off pieces of the dough and shape them into 2½ to 3 dozen golf ball–size pieces.

4. Mix the brown sugar, white sugar, and cinnamon together in a small bowl.

5. One at a time, dip the dough balls into the melted butter, roll them in the sugar mixture, and place them in the prepared pan. Stack the balls on top of one another until the pan is full.

6. Bake the sticky bread for 20 to 25 minutes. You can tell if the bread is ready by sticking a toothpick into it. If the toothpick comes out clean, the bread is done baking. Set the bread aside to cool for about 10 minutes.

7. Use a small spatula to gently loosen the bread from the sides of the pan. Now it's time to turn the sticky bread out of the pan. First place a serving dish facedown on top of the fluted tube pan. Next hold the dish and pan together securely, and flip them over. Slowly lift the pan off the plate and release the sticky bread.

8. Let the bread cool slightly. Then pull pieces from it, and enjoy!

Minnie's Baked Caramel French Toast

(Serves 10)

Calories: 150   Total Fat: 5 grams   Total Carbohydrate: 20 grams   Fiber: 1 gram   Protein: 6 grams

Ingredients:

Small (10 oz.) loaf wheat-free bread, pulled apart into 1-inch pieces

⅓ cup brown sugar

¾ tsp. cinnamon

Dash of salt

6 large eggs

1¼ cups milk

1 tsp. vanilla extract

Allergy Substitution Note:

In case of egg allergy, use egg substitute.

In case of milk allergy, use dairy-free milk.

This sweet French toast dish is a big hit with Minnie's friends. It's sure to be a hit with yours, too!

Directions:

1. Generously butter a 9- x 13-inch casserole dish. Place the bread pieces in the dish.

2. In a small bowl, mix together the brown sugar, cinnamon, and salt. Sprinkle the mixture over the bread.

3. In a mixing bowl, whisk together the eggs, milk, and vanilla extract. Pour the egg mixture evenly over the bread. Then use a spatula to press the bread down to make sure it is well coated.

4. Cover the baking pan with aluminum foil and refrigerate it for at least 4 hours or overnight.

5. When you're ready to cook the French toast, heat the oven to 350°F. Bake the French toast with the foil in place for 20 minutes. Remove the foil, and continue baking for another 25 minutes.

6. Take the tray out of the oven and let cool for about 5 minutes before serving.

TIP To change it up, try using a loaf of wheat-free raisin bread.

Scout's Pumpkin Chocolate Chip Muffins

(Makes 12 muffins)

Calories: 210   Total Fat: 8 grams   Total Carbohydrate: 35 grams   Fiber: 1 gram   Protein: 1 gram

Made with yummy chocolate bits, these perfectly spiced muffins are one of Scout's favorite on-the-go treats.

Ingredients:

1 cup pumpkin puree

⅓ cup vegetable oil

2 tsp. baking powder mixed with 3 Tbsp. water

1¼ cup sugar

1¼ cup rice flour

1 tsp. baking powder

2 tsp. pumpkin pie spice

½ tsp. baking soda

½ tsp. salt

½ cup dairy- and wheat-free mini chocolate chips (such as Enjoy Life® Semi-Sweet Chocolate Mini Chips), plus extra for topping (optional)

Directions:

1. Preheat the oven to 350°F. Grease a muffin tin or line with paper liners.

2. In a large bowl, mix together pumpkin puree, vegetable oil, baking soda and water mixture, and sugar until well blended.

3. In another bowl, whisk together the flour, baking powder, pumpkin pie spice, baking soda, and salt. Add to the pumpkin mixture and whisk until just combined. Fold in the chocolate chips.

TIP These muffins are great fresh, but they freeze well, too! Just pull one out of the freezer and thaw for a quick snack!

4. Spoon batter into prepared muffin tin, filling each about ⅔ full. Sprinkle a few more chips on top of the muffins.

5. Bake for 25 to 30 minutes or until a toothpick inserted in the middle of a muffin comes out clean. Cool in the pan for 5 minutes, then transfer muffins to a cooling rack.

Minnie and Daisy's Classic Winter Porridge

(Serves 4 – Serving size ½ cup)

Calories: 550   Total Fat: 6 grams   Total Carbohydrate: 105 grams   Fiber: 9 grams   Protein: 18 grams

Minnie and Daisy love playing in the snow. When they get too cold, they warm up with a warm bowl of spiced porridge with brown sugar and dried fruits.

Ingredients:

4 cups milk

2 cups old-fashioned oats

1½ cups dried fruit mix (like raisins, cranberries, and apricots)

1½ tsp. cinnamon

½ tsp. ground ginger

¼ tsp. ground nutmeg

¼ tsp. ground cloves or allspice

1½ tsp. vanilla extract

¼ cup brown sugar

2 cups water

Allergy Substitution Note:

In case of milk allergy, use dairy-free milk.

Directions:

1. Warm the milk over medium heat in a large saucepan. Stir in the oats and cook for about 5 minutes, stirring constantly.

2. Stir in the fruit, spices, vanilla extract, brown sugar, and water. Turn the heat down to medium-low and simmer for 5 more minutes.

3. Portion out into 4 individual bowls. Top with additional dried fruit if desired.

TIP

Add a Tbsp. of your favorite jam for different flavors!

Clean Out that Pantry!

Organizing your fridge and cabinets to make them more allergy-friendly can seem overwhelming, but it won't be as tough with these great ideas.

1. **Do a clean sweep.** Get a fresh start by removing everything from your cabinets and fridge; just make sure that those with severe food allergies aren't around while you do it. Remove shelf liners, scrub every nook and cranny, and replace with plastic liners that can be sanitized in the dishwasher.

2. **Figure out what to keep.** Decide if you want to have foods that contain your child's allergens in your home (for family members without allergies to eat). Some families do; others don't.

3. **Check expiration dates.** If any food in your kitchen has expired, throw it away. If your child gets sick, you don't want to question whether it was due to expired food or a potential allergen.

4. **Sort the food.** If you're getting rid of all foods with allergens, put them in a box and donate to friends or a food bank. Then start a pile with things that everybody can eat. In another pile, away from the allergen-free foods, place foods that are questionable, meaning that you have to read labels closely or call the manufacturer. (This is a time-consuming task, so if you want to set aside time to do this later, place these foods in a box out of reach of children with severe allergies.)

5. **Add labels.** If you decide to keep foods that aren't safe for someone in your home, label them carefully! Try using a red sticker with the name of the person who shouldn't eat the food or what the food contains that is a potential allergen. Visit **www.MyAllergyKingdom.com** for great printable stickers!

6. **Designate sections.** Start by allocating an area, such as a few shelves, for foods the whole family can eat. Then create sections for each family member who has a severe food allergy. To separate packaged foods, plastic containers are fine. But for loose items, opt for stainless steel or glass containers, which are less porous—so crumbs are less likely to seep into the cracks. Consider using color-coded lids or bowls to store the "safe foods" as a way to keep everyone on the same page. You can also use shallow bins to store foods such as dairy-free yogurt and spreads in the refrigerator.

7. **Organize at the store.** Now that you've set up your kitchen, make your grocery shopping just as allergy-friendly. Rule number one: read all food labels. Also bag your own groceries, keeping allergen-containing foods separate. Once you get home, read the food labels again to make sure you are storing everything in the proper place.

8. **Keep it up.** Maintain your pantry by repeating the first few steps monthly or every other month. Be especially sure to keep an eye out for loose crumbs and expired foods!

Lunch

Minnie's Ribbon Swirl Salad

(Serves 2)

Calories: 60   Total Fat: 30 grams   Total Carbohydrate: 8 grams   Fiber: 2 grams   Protein: 2 grams

Being the fashionable mouse that she is, Minnie is a pro at tying bows. But that's not all—she can even weave veggie ribbons into a stylish side.

Ingredients:

1 seedless cucumber, scrubbed

Bowl of ice water

1 medium carrot, scrubbed and peeled

1 Tbsp. of your favorite salad dressing

Allergy note:
Be sure to read the ingredients on your salad dressing to make sure it is allergen-free.

Directions:

1. Slice the ends off the cucumber and discard them. Then cut the cucumber into 8-inch sections. Use a vegetable peeler to slice ribbons from each section, and put them into the bowl of ice water.

2. Prepare the carrot as you did the cucumber, adding the ribbons to the bowl.

3. Let the ribbons soak in the water for 15 to 20 minutes to crisp them up. Then drain them in a colander. Dry the bowl, and put the ribbons back in it. Drizzle on the salad dressing, toss, and serve.

Mickey's Sweet and Sassy Salad

(Serves 2)

Calculated using blueberries
Calories: 90   Total Fat: 0 grams   Total Carbohydrate: 20 grams   Fiber: 6 grams   Protein: 5 grams

Orange Ginger Dressing
Calories: 80   Total Fat: 4.5 grams   Total Carbohydrate: 11 grams   Fiber: 0 grams   Protein: 0 grams

Topped with homemade citrus dressing, this salad combines the fruits and vegetables Mickey likes best. It's the perfect lunch to share with friends.

Ingredients:

10–12 oz. leafy green lettuce

1 cup grated carrot

1 cucumber, sliced

¼ cup fresh peas

¼ cup fresh blueberries and/or raspberries

Orange Ginger Dressing:

⅓ cup orange juice

2 tsp. lemon juice

2 tsp. canola oil

2 tsp. honey

⅛ tsp. ground ginger

⅛ tsp. salt

Directions:

1. Rinse the lettuce well with cold water and then pat the leaves dry with paper towels. Tear the lettuce into bite-size pieces, and put some on each salad plate.

2. Top the lettuce with some grated carrot, several cucumber slices, and a spoonful of fresh peas. Add several berries.

3. In a small bowl, whisk together the citrus dressing ingredients. Spoon dressing onto each salad, and serve.

Minnie's Cucumber Salad

(Serves 2)

Calories: 80   Total Fat: 2.5 grams   Total Carbohydrate: 11 grams   Fiber: 2 grams   Protein: 3 grams

Minnie loves growing cucumbers in her garden. They make the perfect ingredient for this tasty salad.

Ingredients:

1 medium cucumber

3 Tbsp. rice wine vinegar

1 Tbsp. sugar

Salt to taste

Dash crushed red pepper flakes (optional)

Directions:

1. Cut the cucumber into thin circular slices.

2. In a medium-size bowl, stir together the cucumber slices, vinegar, sugar, and salt. Add the crushed red pepper flakes if you're using them.

3. Chill the cucumber salad for 30 minutes before serving.

TIP Red pepper flakes are really spicy, so don't use too many—unless you want to breathe fire!

Daisy's Pasta Shell Salad

(Serves 8 – Serving size: ½ cup)

Calories: 350   Total Fat: 13 grams   Total Carbohydrate: 46 grams   Fiber: 1 grams   Protein: 6 grams

This colorful combination of garden veggies and shell-shaped pasta is the perfect mix of land and sea.

Ingredients:

1 (16 oz.) box of wheat-free pasta shells

½ cup diced red bell pepper

½ cup shredded carrots

½ cup halved cherry tomatoes

¼ cup grated Parmesan cheese

2 Tbsp. snipped chives

1 cup Italian salad dressing

¼ tsp. salt

¼ tsp. ground pepper

Allergy Substitution Note:

In case of milk allergy, use dairy-free cheese.
Be sure to check salad dressing ingredients for allergens.

TIP Cubed mozzarella cheese and pepperoni slices make great additions to this salad. Your favorite grilled meat would also make a great addition.

Directions:

1. Prepare the pasta according to the directions on the box.

2. In a large bowl, combine the cooked pasta shells, red pepper, carrots, cherry tomatoes, Parmesan, and chives. Stir with a wooden spoon to mix them.

3. Pour the Italian salad dressing over the pasta, and sprinkle on the salt and pepper. Stir again until all the ingredients are evenly coated.

4. Cover the bowl with plastic wrap and chill until serving time.

Mickey's Corn Chowder

(Serves 8 – Serving size: 1 cup)

Calories: 150   Total Fat: 6 grams   Total Carbohydrate: 25 grams   Fiber: 3 grams   Protein: 5 grams

Topped with bits of bacon, this hearty soup is one of Mickey's favorite ways to warm up on a cold day!

Ingredients:

1 medium onion

2 medium red potatoes

2 Tbsp. butter

1 cup water

2 cups whole-kernel corn

1½ cups creamed corn

1½ cups milk

½ tsp. salt

Dash of pepper

5 Tbsp. bacon bits

Allergy Substitution Note:

In case of milk allergy, use milk alternative and dairy-free margarine.

Be sure to check creamed corn ingredients for allergens.

TIP Try this soup with a nice wheat-free bread for a delicious combination.

Directions:

1. Peel off the onion's hard outer layer, and cut the onion into ½-inch pieces. Then chop the red potatoes into bite-size cubes. Set the onion and potatoes aside.

2. Melt the butter in a heavy saucepan over medium-low heat. Cook the onion in the melted butter until the onion starts to turn clear (about 3 or 4 minutes).

3. Add the potatoes and water, then cover the pan and let simmer for 15 minutes.

4. Stir in the whole-kernel corn, creamed corn, milk, salt, and pepper. Continue cooking and stirring the chowder until it heats through (about 7 minutes).

5. Ladle the chowder into bowls, sprinkle bacon bits on top, and serve.

Minnie's Polka-Dot Tomato Soup

(Serves 4 - Serving size: approximately 1 cup)

Calculated using American cheese

Calories: 130   Total Fat: 9 grams   Total Carbohydrate: 17 grams   Fiber: 2 grams   Protein: 3 grams

Ingredients:

2 slices of cheese (American or provolone)

1 (14.75 oz.) can creamed corn

1 (14.5 oz.) can diced fire-roasted tomatoes

1 Tbsp. butter

Salt and pepper to taste

Allergy Substitution Note:

In case of milk allergy, use dairy-free cheese and dairy-free margarine.

Be sure to check creamed corn ingredients for allergens.

Leave it to Minnie to serve soup with style. This creamy tomato and corn blend, topped with melted cheese polka dots, is one of her specialties.

Directions:

1. Use a small round cookie cutter to cut a bunch of circular "polka dots" from the sliced cheese. (If you don't have a small cookie cutter, any circular object with a raised edge will do. Even plastic bottle caps are perfect for this recipe!) Set the cheesy polka dots aside for now.

2. Combine the corn and diced tomatoes in a blender, and blend them until smooth.

3. Pour the mixture into a medium saucepan. Bring the mixture to a slow simmer over medium-low heat.

4. Add the butter, salt, and pepper, and continue heating the soup, stirring all the while. Heat until the butter melts and blends evenly into the mixture.

5. Ladle the soup into serving bowls, and immediately top it with the cheese polka dots. Wait a minute or so for the cheese to soften and melt around the edges before serving.

Scout's Friendship Soup

(Serves 4 - Serving size: 1 cup)

Calculated using white rice

Calories: 110   Total Fat: 2 grams   Total Carbohydrate: 9 grams   Fiber: 1 gram   Protein: 13 grams

Made with seven tasty ingredients, this recipe adds up to one delicious meal for you and your friends.

Ingredients:

1 carrot

2 stalks celery

1 qt. chicken broth

1 cooked chicken breast, cut into small pieces (about 1 packed cup)

½ cup uncooked wheat-free pasta or rice

Salt and pepper to taste

Allergy Note:

Be sure to check the ingredients in the chicken broth for allergens.

Directions:

1. Peel the carrot and cut it into thin slices. Prepare your celery stalks by slicing off the leafy tops and white bottoms. Cut the remaining stalks into thin slices.

2. Combine the chicken broth, carrot slices, and celery slices in a large saucepan. Cook over high heat until the broth begins to bubble. Turn the heat down to low and let simmer for 3 minutes.

3. Stir in the chicken and pasta or rice. Continue simmering the soup until the pasta/rice is cooked al dente (about 10 more minutes).

4. Season the soup with salt and ground pepper, and serve.

TIP For a simpler soup, bring the broth to a simmer and stir in 1 cup frozen mixed vegetables in place of the carrot and celery.

Goofy's Cowboy Chili

(Serves 8 - Serving size: 1 cup)

Calculated using stewed tomatoes and cheese
Calories: 270   Total Fat: 7 grams   Total Carbohydrate: 27 grams   Fiber: 7 grams   Protein: 25 grams

What is a cowboy's favorite meal? This simple chili that tastes even better the next day, if it lasts that long!

Ingredients:

1 lb. lean ground beef

1 cup onion, chopped

1 (14.5 oz.) can stewed or roasted tomatoes

1 (8 oz.) can tomato sauce

1 (15 oz.) can dark red kidney beans, drained

1 (15 oz.) can light red kidney beans, drained

1 (14 oz.) can beef broth

2 tsp. garlic powder

1 tsp. salt

½ tsp. pepper

1 cup cheddar cheese, shredded (optional)

Allergy Substitution

Note:
In case of milk allergy, use dairy-free cheese or eliminate cheese altogether.
Be sure to check beef broth for all allergens.

Directions:

1. Place the beef and onion in a large pot. Cook them over medium-high heat until the meat is brown and the onions are tender.

2. Add the remaining ingredients, except for the cheddar cheese, to the pot. Stir, bring to a boil, and reduce heat to low.

3. Cover partially and let simmer for 30 to 45 minutes (the longer it simmers, the thicker your chili will be).

4. Serve with a sprinkling of shredded cheddar cheese if you like.

Donald's Tasty Sandwiches

(Makes 8 to 12)

Calculated based on 1 sandwich

Calories: 380   Total Fat: 21 grams   Total Carbohydrate: 35 grams   Fiber: 3 grams   Protein: 12 grams

Ingredients:

1 Tbsp. mayonnaise

¼ tsp. garlic powder

¼ tsp. paprika

Wheat-free bread of two different colors

Sliced ham

Sliced cheese

Allergy Substitution Note:

In case of milk allergy, use dairy-free cheese.

In case of egg allergy, use an egg-free mayonnaise.

In case of soy allergy, replace mayonnaise with mustard.

 TIP You can make any shape sandwich you want by using different cookie cutters.

Donald loves making these flower-shaped sandwiches for Daisy. To make them extra tasty, he seasons the mayonnaise with a few secret ingredients.

Directions:

1. In a small bowl, stir together the mayonnaise, garlic powder, and paprika.

2. For each sandwich, use a large flower-shaped cookie cutter (about 3 inches wide) to cut the center from 2 slices of wheat-free bread.

3. Use a small round cookie cutter (about 1 ¼ inches wide) to cut a hole in the middle of each bread flower cutout. Place the center of the lighter-colored flower into the darker-colored flower and the center of the darker-colored flower into the lighter-colored flower.

4. Cut flower shapes from slices of ham and cheese (but don't cut holes in the centers).

5. Spread mayonnaise mixture on one of the bread flowers, and layer on the ham and cheese cutouts. Top off the sandwich with the second bread flower. You can spread a little more mayonnaise on this layer, too, if you like.

Mickey Mouse Club Sandwich

(Serves 2)

Calories: 280   Total Fat: 16 grams   Total Carbohydrate: 21 grams   Fiber: 1 grams   Protein: 11 grams

Ingredients:

2 Tbsp. mayonnaise

¼ tsp. onion powder

¼ tsp. celery salt

3 slices of wheat-free bread

2 lettuce leaves

3 turkey slices

3 tomato slices

3 strips of cooked bacon

Allergy Substitution Note:

In case of egg allergy, use an egg-free mayonnaise.

In case of soy allergy, replace mayonnaise with mustard.

There's nothing Mickey likes to eat more for lunch than sandwiches. Stuffed with turkey, bacon, and fresh veggies, this double-decker sure fits the bill!

Directions:

1. In a small bowl, stir together the mayonnaise, onion powder, and celery salt.

2. Toast the bread. Spread a light coating of the seasoned mayonnaise on one of the slices. Then top it with a lettuce leaf and the turkey slices.

3. Set the second slice of toast on top, and press down lightly. Spread a little more mayonnaise on top of the toast and then layer the tomato slices, bacon, and second lettuce leaf.

4. Spread mayonnaise on the third toast slice, and place it (coated side down) on top of the sandwich. Press down lightly to stick the sandwich fillings together.

5. Cut the sandwich into 4 triangles, and poke a toothpick down through the center of each triangle. Place 2 of the triangles on each serving plate.

Lifestyle Tip: Food Planning for School

School can be a challenging environment for a child with food allergies. Other parents and students might not know about a child's allergy or fully understand the severity of food allergies. Here are a few tips that can help make school a safe and fun place for children with allergies.

- **Meet with the school nurse and your child's teacher before the start of the school year.** They are responsible for your child's safety while he or she is at school, so it's important that they understand your child's food allergy, including what your child can and cannot eat, all parts of your Anaphylaxis Action Plan (Allergy Action Plan), and how your child can be safely included in school activities. Ask your child's teacher to prevent outside food from being brought into the classroom. If this is not possible, work with the teacher to create a game plan for birthday celebrations and holiday parties where food might be brought in. If your child will be eating in a cafeteria, find out who will be monitoring mealtime and ensure that they are also aware of your Anaphylaxis Action Plan.

- **Ask your child's teacher to send out a letter about food allergies at the start of the school year.** Sometimes parents of kids without food allergies don't understand how dangerous food can be for a child with food allergies. A letter that talks about the specific food allergies of kids in the classroom, what snacks are acceptable, and the symptoms of a severe allergic reaction can help avoid dangerous accidents.

- **Find out where your child will eat.** Ask the school if there is a policy on food allergies. If there's an allergen-free table in the cafeteria, it should be separate but not isolating. Make sure that it's not close to the vending machines and highly trafficked areas (say, next to the trash cans). The table should also be near an exit, in case your child needs to quickly leave (for example, in case of a food fight). Ask if there will be signs to warn others that the area needs to remain allergen-free. Be sure to ask if the table will be properly sanitized with a disposable rag and bucket designated for that table only. As an extra safety precaution, remind your child to place his or her lunch on a napkin or eat directly out of a lunch box. It's also a good idea to send your child to school with allergen-free meals and snacks instead of having them buy food from the cafeteria. You may also want to ask the school whether you can supply safe snacks to keep on hand in case of a special occasion or holiday. Sending your child in with allergen-free food will ensure that they do not eat anything that will cause an allergic reaction.

- **Make sure your child has access to his or her epinephrine auto-injector** if one has been prescribed by your doctor and that he or she knows who to go to in case of a reaction. During the first week and occasionally throughout the year, follow up with the school to see if any changes need to be made to your Action Plan, and check the expiration date of your epinephrine auto-injector. That's also the perfect time to let the staff know how much you appreciate all they're doing to protect your child.

Be sure your child understands the importance of not trading his or her food with other classmates. You may want to provide your child's teacher with special treats your child can eat in case of a party or unplanned event that he or she feels like part of the celebration.

Snacks and Drinks

Minnie's Lemon Carrots

(Serves 3 - Serving size: ½ cup)

Calories: 80   Total Fat: 4 grams   Total Carbohydrate: 13 grams   Fiber: 2 grams   Protein: 1 gram

Ingredients:

3 large carrots

½ cup water

1 Tbsp. butter

1 Tbsp. honey

1 tsp. fresh lemon juice

Dash of salt

Allergy Substitution Note:
In case of milk allergy, use dairy-free margarine.

With carrots fresh from her garden, Minnie loves sharing this snack with her friends!

Directions:

1. Scrub and peel the carrots. Cut off and discard the tops and tips. Then cut the carrots into ¼-inch slices.

2. Combine the carrot slices, water, butter, and honey in a medium-size frying pan. Bring the mixture to a boil. Then turn the heat down just enough to cook the carrots at a low boil, stirring occasionally to evenly distribute the butter and honey.

3. When most of the water has evaporated and the carrots are just tender enough to poke a fork through, stir in the lemon juice and salt.

4. Turn the heat down to low, and cook the carrots for another minute or so before serving.

Goofy's Snow Peas

(Serves 4 - Serving size: ¼ cup)

Calories: 30   Total Fat: 1 gram   Total Carbohydrate: 4 grams   Fiber: 1 gram   Protein: 1 gram

Goofy loves these tasty snow peas as a snack at home or when he's on the go!

Ingredients:

½ lb. snow peas

1 Tbsp. water

1 tsp. butter

Allergy Substitution Note:

In case of milk allergy, use dairy-free margarine in place of butter.

 TIP For a zestier dish, drizzle ½ tsp. or so of Italian dressing on the snow peas instead of butter.

Directions:

1. Rinse the snow peas well in cold water. Then snap off the top of each pod, pulling it downward to remove the strings along the sides.

2. Place the prepared pods and the Tbsp. of water in a microwavable casserole dish. Cover the dish, and microwave the peas on high for 3 minutes.

3. Use potholders to remove the casserole dish from the microwave. Add butter to the peas, gently stir, and serve.

Scout's Homemade Hummus

(Serves 4)

Calculated for dip only

Calories: 270   Total Fat: 16 grams   Total Carbohydrate: 25 grams   Fiber: 7 grams   Protein: 8 grams

Flavored with lemon and garlic, this tasty chickpea spread is a staple in Scout's kitchen.

Ingredients:

1 (15 oz.) can garbanzo beans

¼ cup olive oil

2 Tbsp. lemon juice

¼ tsp. garlic powder

¼ tsp. salt

Rice crackers or fresh vegetables

Directions:

1. Drain the garbanzo beans and combine with the olive oil, lemon juice, garlic powder, and salt in the bowl of a food processor or blender.

2. Blend ingredients until smooth.

3. Spoon the hummus into a small bowl. Serve with rice crackers or fresh veggies!

TIP There are lots of fun ways to eat hummus. Try it on pretzels, corn tortillas—even bagels!

Donald's Sweet Potato Coins

(Serves 2)

Calories: 170   Total Fat: 7 grams   Total Carbohydrate: 26 grams   Fiber: 4 grams   Protein: 2 grams

Ingredients:

2 medium-size sweet potatoes, peeled and sliced about ¼-inch thick

1 Tbsp. vegetable oil or olive oil

Salt and pepper to taste

These sweet-and-salty oven fries remind Donald of treasure hunting with his nephews. But these coins are much tastier!

Directions:

1. Heat the oven to 400°F. Use a small round cookie cutter (up to 2 inches wide or so) to cut out a bunch of "coins" from the sweet potato slices. To make it extra easy, place the flat end of a wooden spoon on top of the cutter, and press down on the spoon.

2. Put the potato coins in a mixing bowl. Drizzle the oil on top, and stir with a wooden spoon until the coins are evenly coated.

3. Line a baking sheet with aluminum foil. Then place the coins on the sheet, spacing them slightly apart. Sprinkle on salt and pepper.

4. Bake the coins until the bottoms are golden brown, about 10 to 12 minutes. Remove them from the oven, and use a spatula to flip them over. Bake the coins for another 10 to 12 minutes.

 TIP You can use different cookie cutters, such as stars or hearts, to make fun shapes, too!

Minnie's Pink Popcorn

(Serves 3)

Calories: 210   Total Fat: 15 grams   Total Carbohydrate: 20 grams   Fiber: 1 gram   Protein: 2 grams

As far as Minnie is concerned, everything looks better in pink!

Ingredients:

Bag of popped microwave popcorn (about 6 cups)

2½ Tbsp. butter

18 large marshmallows

3 Tbsp. strawberry-flavored gelatin powder

Allergy Substitution Note:

In case of milk allergy, use dairy-free margarine in place of butter.

Some marshmallows contain eggs. Check the ingredients in case of an egg allergy.

Directions:

1. Put the popped popcorn in a large mixing bowl, removing any unpopped kernels.

2. Melt the butter in a medium-size saucepan over medium-low heat. Add the marshmallows and stir continually until they melt and turn into a smooth sauce. Stir in the strawberry gelatin powder. Use a plastic spoon for this step. (The pink gelatin can stain a wooden spoon.)

3. Immediately pour the pink marshmallow over the popcorn, and gently stir to evenly cover the popcorn.

4. Let the popcorn cool for a few minutes before serving.

TIP Melted marshmallow is hot, so be sure to use a long-handled spoon to stir it. And remember, don't lick the spoon until it cools down!

Triple-licious Fruit Salad

(Serves 6)

Calories: 25   Total Fat: 0 grams   Total Carbohydrate: 7 grams   Fiber: 1 gram   Protein: 1 gram

There's nothing Huey, Dewey, and Louie like to stir up more than trouble—except maybe this sweet and juicy tricolored treat.

Ingredients:

Half a cantaloupe

Half a honeydew melon

Half a small seedless watermelon

Directions:

1. Use a melon baller to scoop 1 dozen balls from each melon half, and combine them all in a big bowl.

2. Gently stir the melon balls with a wooden spoon so that the colors are evenly mixed.

3. Spoon your fruit salad into small serving dishes, and enjoy! Cover any leftover fruit salad with plastic wrap, and chill it in the refrigerator until you're ready for more.

TIP This summertime salad is even more refreshing when served with snipped mint.

Daisy's Jitterbug Juice

(Serves 2)

Calories: 90   Total Fat: 0 grams   Total Carbohydrate: 22 grams   Fiber: 0 grams   Protein: 0 grams

A dazzling dancer like Daisy can really work up a thirst. When it comes to refreshments, this fizzy fruit drink is her top choice.

Ingredients:

1 cup unsweetened pineapple juice

½ cup lemonade

1 cup seltzer water

Ice

2 lemon slices

Directions:

1. Stir the pineapple juice and lemonade together in a pitcher or quart-size measuring cup.

2. Slowly pour in the seltzer water.

3. Pour the juice mixture into tall glasses filled with ice. Add a lemon slice to each glass, and serve.

Mickey's Raspberry Mint Iced Tea

(Serves 4 - Serving size: 1 cup)

Calories: 50   Total Fat: 0 grams   Total Carbohydrate: 14 grams   Fiber: 0 grams   Protein: 0 grams

When the weather's warm, Mickey helps everyone keep cool with his delicious iced tea.

Ingredients:

1 qt. water

3 bags herbal raspberry tea

2 bags herbal mint tea

3 Tbsp. honey

Ice

Directions:

1. On the stove, heat the water until it is near boiling. Then remove from heat.
2. Steep the bags of raspberry and mint tea in the water for 4 minutes.
3. Remove the tea bags and stir in the honey while the tea is still warm. Let the sweetened tea cool.
4. Fill tall glasses with plenty of ice, pour in the tea, and serve.

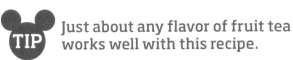 Just about any flavor of fruit tea works well with this recipe.

Goofy's Sun Punch

(Serves 4 - Serving size 1 cup)

Calories: 60   Total Fat: 0 grams   Total Carbohydrate: 14 grams   Fiber: 0 grams   Protein: 0 grams

This golden-yellow drink is bright and sparkly—just like Goofy!

Ingredients:

1 cup lemonade

1 cup orange juice

2 cups seltzer water

Ice

Directions:

1. Stir the lemonade and orange juice together in a pitcher.

2. Slowly pour in the seltzer water.

3. Fill 4 tall glasses with plenty of ice. Pour in the punch, and serve.

 **TIP** For a festive touch, add a slice of orange or lemon to each glass.

Minnie's Sweet Smoothie

(Serves 1)

Calories: 390   Total Fat: 9 grams   Total Carbohydrate: 70 grams   Fiber: 3 grams   Protein: 7 grams

Flavored with lime and banana, this frothy smoothie is perfect for warm summer days.

Ingredients:

1 banana

½ cup water

1 cup vanilla frozen yogurt

1 Tbsp. lime juice

Allergy Substitution Note:

In case of milk allergy, use non-dairy ice cream or lime Italian ice in place of frozen yogurt. If you prefer a fruit smoothie, replace yogurt with frozen fruit, and use 2 frozen bananas in place of the single banana!

Directions:

1. Break the banana into pieces and put them in a blender.

2. Add the water, frozen yogurt, and lime juice.

3. Blend the ingredients until they are smooth and creamy.

4. Pour the smoothie into a tall glass, and serve with a straw.

 TIP For a sweet switch, try making this smoothie with fresh-squeezed lemon or orange juice instead of lime juice.

On-the-Go Snacks:

Store-bought snacks are great, but remember to check the ingredient lists for your child's allergens. Here are some ideas to get you started!

- Apples
- Baby carrots
- Celery sticks
- Cherry tomatoes
- Cheese sticks (for those with a dairy/soy allergy, you can find dairy-free and soy-free cheese sticks)
- Dried fruit
- Fruit cups
- Peppers
- Popcorn (varies by brand, check the packaging)
- Pretzels (varies by brand, check the packaging)
- Yogurt (dairy-free or soy-free if applicable)
- Veggie chips (varies by brand, check the packaging)

It's always good to have snacks on hand that are allergy friendly. Here's a list of some on-the-go snack ideas.

Dinner

Scout's Smashed Potatoes

(Serves 6)

Calories: 410   Total Fat: 19 grams   Total Carbohydrate: 54 grams   Fiber: 6 grams   Protein: 6 grams

Ingredients:

1–2 tsp. kosher salt

Ground pepper, to taste

½ cup extra virgin olive oil

12 small potatoes (such as red bliss)

Have fun smashing these roasted potatoes to make a great easy side for any meal.

Directions:

1. Fill a large pot with water, add about 1 tsp. of salt, and then add the potatoes. Set the pot over high heat until the water begins to boil, then turn the heat down to medium-low and let it simmer for about 20 minutes, or until the potatoes feel soft when you insert a fork.

2. Preheat the oven to 450°F. While the potatoes cook, line a baking pan with aluminum foil and coat it with cooking spray. Carefully remove the potatoes from the water, and arrange them on the pan so they are evenly spaced.

3. Let your child join in the fun by using the bottom of a glass to press down on each potato and smash it. Once all the potatoes are smashed, drizzle them with olive oil and season with salt and pepper.

4. Place the baking pan on the top rack in the oven, and roast the potatoes for 20 to 25 minutes or until crispy and brown at the edges. Remove from the oven and let them cool down before you enjoy them!

TIP If you're short on time, you can boil and smash these potatoes the night before and store them in the refrigerator. The next day, just let the potatoes come to room temperature before placing them in the oven.

Goofy's Confetti Corn

(Serves 4 - Serving size: ½ cup)

Calories: 130   Total Fat: .5 grams   Total Carbohydrate: 18 grams   Fiber: 3 grams   Protein: 5 grams

Made with red pepper, yellow corn, and fresh green basil, this colorful medley makes a festive addition to any meal!

Ingredients:

1 tsp. vegetable oil

½ cup diced red bell pepper

2 cups cooked corn

3 strips cooked bacon, crumbled

1 tsp. dried basil

½ tsp. butter

Salt and pepper to taste

Allergy Substitution Note:

In case of milk allergy, use dairy-free margarine in place of butter.

Directions:

1. Heat the vegetable oil in a medium-size frying pan over medium-low heat. Sauté the diced red pepper in the oil for 2 minutes.

2. Add the corn, crumbled bacon, basil, and butter. Stir the ingredients together, and cook them until they are hot and well mixed and the butter is melted.

3. Remove the pan from the heat. Stir in salt and pepper to taste, and serve.

TIP Leftover cooked sweet corn, cut off the cob, tastes especially good in this recipe.

Donald's Moo Shu

(Serves 6)

Calories: 160   Total Fat: 6 grams   Total Carbohydrate: 9 grams   Fiber: 2 grams   Protein: 18 grams

Donald likes to have plenty to eat! This delicious dish is fun *and* filling!

Ingredients:

3 tsp. vegetable oil

1 tsp. ginger powder

4 cups broccoli slaw mix

1 lb. pork tenderloin, cooked and sliced

¼ cup hoisin sauce

Salt to taste

Corn tortillas, warmed

Allergy Substitution Note:

In case of soy allergy, remove hoisin sauce from recipe. Some hoisin sauces contain wheat starch or flour. Be sure to check the ingredients before use.

Directions:

1. Heat the oil in a large, nonstick frying pan or wok over medium-high heat. Add the ginger powder and stir for 1 minute.

2. Add the broccoli slaw to the pan, and turn up the heat a little. Stir-fry the vegetables for 4 to 5 minutes. Cook them just long enough to darken in color without losing their crunchiness.

3. Turn the heat down to medium, and stir in the pork and hoisin sauce. Continue cooking the moo shu for another 2 minutes to heat it through. Add salt to taste.

4. When you're ready to eat, spoon some of the moo shu onto the center of a warm tortilla. Then roll or wrap up the tortilla, and enjoy.

TIP You can add a little extra hoisin sauce before serving, if you like.

Mickey's Oh, Boy Tacos

(Makes 8)

Calculated without optional toppings:
Calories: 140   Total Fat: 4.5 grams   Total Carbohydrate: 13 grams   Fiber: 2 grams   Protein: 14 grams

Original optional toppings at 1 Tbsp. each:
Calories: 60   Total Fat: 5 grams   Total Carbohydrate: 1 gram   Fiber: 0 grams   Protein: 2 grams

Ingredients:

1 Tbsp. cornstarch

1 Tbsp. onion powder

1 Tbsp. chili powder

2 Tbsp. garlic powder

2 tsp. cumin

2 tsp. paprika

½ tsp. salt

1 lb. ground beef

1 cup water

8 100% corn taco shells or tortillas

Optional toppings:

Diced fresh tomatoes

Shredded lettuce

Shredded cheddar cheese

Sour cream

Allergy Substitution Note:

In case of milk allergy, use dairy-free cheese and sour cream.

Everyone likes the secret spice blend in Mickey's famous tacos. Whenever his friends hear that tacos are on the menu, they cheer Mickey's signature phrase: Oh, boy!

Directions:

1. In a small bowl, stir together the cornstarch, onion powder, chili powder, garlic powder, cumin, paprika, and salt until evenly blended.

2. Brown the ground beef in a frying pan over medium-low heat. Drain any excess fat from the pan.

3. Add the water and spice blend to the pan, and stir until the beef is evenly coated. Cook the mixture over low heat, stirring occasionally, until it is thick and saucy.

4. Serve the seasoned beef and the remaining ingredients buffet-style so that everyone can fill their own tacos.

Minnie's Yoo-hoo! Stew

(Serves 6)

Calories: 270   Total Fat: 3.5 grams   Total Carbohydrate: 29 grams   Fiber: 3 grams   Protein: 28 grams

Ingredients:

3¼ cups water, divided

1 tsp. salt

2 medium-size red potatoes, scrubbed and diced (about 2 cups)

1 cup frozen corn

1 cup frozen peas

4 cups chicken broth

Whole cooked chicken breast, shredded or chopped into bite-size pieces

¼ tsp. poultry seasoning

3 Tbsp. cornstarch

1 cup mashed potato flakes

Salt and pepper to taste

This saucy chicken and potato stew never fails to be a big hit with Minnie and her crew.

Directions:

1. Combine 3 cups of water, salt, and diced potatoes in a large pot. Bring the water to a low boil, and cook the potatoes until they are just tender enough to break with a fork, about 5 to 7 minutes.

2. Combine the corn and peas in a small colander or strainer and run cold water over them for a minute or so until thawed.

3. Stir the thawed vegetables, chicken broth, shredded chicken, and poultry seasoning into the pot of potatoes and cooking water.

4. Bring the mixture to a boil. Then lower the heat and simmer the stew for 3 to 4 minutes.

5. Pour the remaining ¼ cup of water into a small bowl, and stir in the cornstarch. Pour the dissolved cornstarch into the stew, stirring continuously. Simmer the stew for another 1 to 2 minutes to thicken it.

6. Stir in the mashed potato flakes. Season the stew with salt and pepper, and serve.

Daisy's Amazing Meatloaf

(Serves 6)

Calculated using crushed tomato
Calories: 310   Total Fat: 13 grams   Total Carbohydrate: 23 grams   Fiber: 4 grams   Protein: 27 grams

Ingredients:

1 ½ lbs. 90% lean ground beef

¾ cup regular or instant oatmeal

½ cup dairy-free milk
(such as rice milk)

½ Tbsp. salt

½ tsp. pepper

¼ cup onion, chopped

1 Tbsp. apricot puree

1 (14.5 oz) can diced or
crushed tomato

This hearty meatloaf tastes just like Daisy's mom used to make!

Directions:

1. Preheat oven to 250°F. In a large bowl, mix all ingredients except tomato. Place into a lightly greased loaf pan or shape into a loaf and place in a lightly greased baking dish.

2. Spread diced or crushed tomatoes evenly over the top.

3. Bake for about 2 hours; slice into 6 pieces to serve.

TIP Leftover meatloaf tastes great in a sandwich!

Minnie's Zucchini Spaghetti and Meatballs

(Serves 4)

Calculated using wheat-free bread crumbs and ground turkey

Calories: 320   Total Fat: 14 grams   Total Carbohydrate: 24 grams   Fiber: 3 grams   Protein: 27 grams

Ingredients:

For meatballs:

1 lb. ground chicken or turkey

2 cloves garlic, crushed

1 tsp. onion powder

1 tsp. dried basil

½ tsp. salt

½ tsp. pepper

¼ cup bread crumbs

1 tsp. olive oil

1 (24 oz.) jar pasta sauce

Allergy Substitution Note:

In case of wheat allergy, use bread crumb substitute such as ¾ cup of crushed unsweetened rice flake cereal or 1 cup regular oatmeal.

Be sure to read the ingredients in pasta sauce for allergens.

For zucchini pasta:

4 zucchinis, with or without skin

1 tsp. olive oil

1 tsp. garlic powder

1 tsp. salt

½ tsp. pepper

Minnie loves this healthy meatball recipe. Especially with pasta that comes straight from her garden!

To make the meatballs:

1. Combine the ground chicken or turkey, garlic, onion powder, basil, salt, pepper, and bread crumbs in a large bowl and mix until combined. Roll into small balls and set aside.

2. Heat the olive oil in a large skillet over medium heat. Add the meatballs and brown for 1 minute. Pour in jar of pasta sauce and stir gently to mix. Put on the lid, turn the heat down to low, and allow the meatballs to simmer for 20 minutes.

To make the zucchini pasta:

3. Cut the ends off each zucchini. Using a box grater placed on its side with the largest holes facing up, carefully grate each zucchini lengthwise in long strokes.

4. Heat the olive oil in a skillet over medium-high heat. Add the zucchini, sprinkle with the garlic powder, salt, and pepper, and cook for 2 to 3 minutes or until the "noodles" are cooked through yet firm.

5. Divide the zucchini into 4 bowls, and ladle on a few meatballs and sauce.

Goofy's Grilled Cheese

(Makes 1)

Calories: 320   Total Fat: 19 grams   Total Carbohydrate: 29 grams   Fiber: 1 gram   Protein: 12 grams

Ingredients:

½ Tbsp. butter, softened

2 slices of wheat-free bread

2 slices of cheese (American, cheddar, or provolone)

Dill or bread-and-butter pickles, sliced

Allergy Substitution Note:

In case of milk allergy, use dairy-free margarine in place of butter and dairy-free cheese.

Goofy has a knack for making amazing, if accidental, discoveries—like this wacky grilled cheese with crunchy pickle slices tucked into the middle.

Directions:

1. Spread butter on one side of each bread slice. Flip over one slice so that the buttered side faces down, and top it with a slice of cheese.

2. Use a piece of paper towel to pat the pickles dry and then layer them on the sandwich. Top the pickles with the remaining cheese slice and the second bread slice, this time buttered side up.

3. Heat a small nonstick frying pan over medium heat for 1 minute. Turn the heat down to low, and place the sandwich in the pan. Cover the pan, and grill the sandwich for 2½ minutes.

4. Use a spatula to flip the sandwich, and gently but firmly press down on the top. Re-cover the pan, and continue grilling the sandwich until the cheese is melted and the flip side is browned (another 2 to 3 minutes).

5. Transfer the grilled sandwich to a plate, slice it in half, and serve.

Minnie's Easy Pea-sy Bow Ties and Cheese

(Serves 4)

Calories: 370   Total Fat: 14 grams   Total Carbohydrate: 45 grams   Fiber: 2 grams   Protein: 14 grams

Ingredients:

1 ½ cups uncooked wheat-free bow tie pasta (farfalle)

3 Tbsp. butter

2 Tbsp. wheat-free flour

½ cup chicken broth

1 cup low-fat milk

½ cup shredded or grated Parmesan cheese

1 tsp. onion powder

¼ tsp. garlic powder

¼ tsp. salt

Dash of nutmeg

1 cup frozen peas

Allergy Substitution Note:

In case of milk allergy, use dairy-free margarine in place of butter, dairy-free milk, and dairy-free cheese.

Featuring polka-dot peas and bow tie pasta, Minnie's mac-and-cheese is fancy and flavorful.

Directions:

1. Bring a pot of water to a boil. Stir in pasta and let it cook, setting a timer for 8 minutes.

2. Meanwhile, melt the butter in a small saucepan over medium-low heat. Add the flour and chicken broth, and whisk until the flour dissolves.

3. Stir in the milk, Parmesan cheese, onion powder, garlic powder, salt, and nutmeg. Continue to heat and stir the mixture until the sauce thickens.

4. When the pasta timer goes off, add the frozen peas to the pot of cooking pasta. Cook the pasta for another minute or so until it is done but still firm.

5. Strain the pasta and peas in a colander and then transfer them to a large bowl. Pour on the sauce. Stir until the pasta is evenly coated, and serve.

Scout's Chicken Tenders

(Serves 6)

Calories: 360   Total Fat: 15 grams   Total Carbohydrate: 24 grams   Fiber: 1 gram   Protein: 31 gram

Ingredients:

1 cup crushed potato chips

½ tsp. garlic powder

½ tsp. paprika

¼ tsp. salt

¼ tsp. ground pepper

2 eggs

2 Tbsp. water

1 Tbsp. honey

1 ½ lb. chicken tenders

Allergy Substitution Note:

In case of egg allergy, dip chicken tenders in vegetable oil.

Some potato chips may be fried in peanut oil. Be sure to read ingredients carefully before using.

 TIP Serve your chicken tenders with honey mustard or barbecue sauce for dipping.

Scout doesn't know much about cooking. Luckily, this scrumptious recipe is so easy even he can make it!

Directions:

1. Heat the oven to 400°F. Line a baking sheet with parchment paper.
2. Combine the potato chips, garlic powder, paprika, salt, and pepper in a sealable, gallon-size plastic bag.
3. In a medium-size bowl, whisk together the eggs, water, and honey.
4. Rinse the chicken tenders with cold water and then pat them dry with paper towels. Place the tenders in the egg mixture so that they are completely covered.
5. Use a fork to transfer 2 or 3 tenders to the bag with the potato chip mixture. Seal the bag, and shake. Arrange the coated chicken pieces on the baking sheet. Repeat this step until all the tenders are coated and on the sheet.
6. Bake the chicken for 10 minutes. Then turn the pieces over and continue baking until they are cooked through (another 10 minutes or so).

Daisy's Shepherd's Pie

(Serves 8)

Calories: 290   Total Fat: 12 grams   Total Carbohydrate: 25 grams   Fiber: 3 grams   Protein: 20 grams

Ingredients:

2 Tbsp. butter

1 medium onion, chopped

1 stalk celery, chopped

1½ lb. ground beef

¼ tsp. garlic powder

3 Tbsp. wheat-free flour

1 cup beef broth

1 (14.5 oz.) can diced tomatoes

1 tsp. dried thyme

½ tsp. dried rosemary

1½ cups corn kernels

5 cups warm mashed potatoes

Paprika

Allergy Substitution Note:

In case of milk allergy, use non-dairy margarine in place of butter.

Daisy loves sharing this tasty treat with all of her friends!

Directions:

1. Melt the butter in a large frying pan over medium heat. Add the onion and celery, and sauté them for 5 minutes, stirring often.

2. Add the ground beef to the pan, and break it up with a wooden spoon or spatula. Cook the meat, stirring and turning it over every so often, until it browns. Then lower the heat, and carefully spoon out any excess fat from the cooking liquid.

3. Stir the garlic and flour into the beef. Add the beef broth, diced tomatoes, thyme, rosemary, and corn. Gently stir all the ingredients until they are well combined.

4. Bring the mixture to a simmer, and cook for 3 to 4 minutes. Then spoon it into a large, greased casserole dish.

5. Heat the oven to 400°F. Spread the warm mashed potatoes on top of the meat and vegetable mixture. Sprinkle the top with paprika.

6. Bake the shepherd's pie until it heats all the way through and the top turns golden brown (about 25 minutes). Let cool for 10 minutes before serving.

 TIP It takes about 6 medium-large potatoes to make 5 cups of mashed potatoes.

Lifestyle Tip: Food Planning for Parties

Parties can be stressful for a child who's managing food allergies. But with the right planning, the anxiety about the food that will be served can be alleviated. Here are a few tips to prepare for a party!

- **Make sure to call the host of the party when you receive the invitation** and talk to him or her about your child's food allergies. Ask about what kinds of food will be served to determine what your child will be able to eat. Make sure the host understands the severity of your child's allergies, and ask that effective cleaning methods be used in food preparation and service.

- **Send your child to the party with separate snacks and treats.** Usually, the host or hostess will want to accommodate your child's allergies and will ask what he or she can do to make them feel included. You may even want to ask the host if you can prepare a dish that is allergen-free for the party. That way your child can eat a safe dish that blends right into the party. However, when it comes to cake or cupcakes, be prepared to send a separate allergy-free treat for your child. Try to provide a food that's the same or at least similar to the foods being served at the party so that your child won't feel different.

- **Show up early.** This will give you time to remind the host or hostess about your child's food allergies. Bring along a kit with your child's epinephrine auto-injectors and your child's Anaphylaxis Action Plan. Make sure to go over your child's Action Plan with the host or hostess, and explain what symptoms to look for in case an allergen is accidentally ingested. If you are leaving your child at the party, give your emergency contact information to the host or hostess, and keep your phone nearby. It is also a good idea to demonstrate how to use your child's auto-injector using a trainer. If you do attend the party, try not to indulge in treats your child can't eat. And remember to try to hang back so your child feels independent.

Relax and remind your child to have fun. Parties should be a fun experience! Try taking the emphasis off the food and remind your child to have fun playing games and celebrating. The less nervous you are, the less nervous your child will be.

Dessert

Huey, Dewey, and Louie's Triple Fruit Crisp

(Serves 8)

Calories: 200   Total Fat: 6 grams   Total Carbohydrate: 34 grams   Fiber: 4 grams   Protein: 1 gram

In honor of his triplet nephews, Donald makes his famous crisp with a trio of tasty fruits—apples, pears, and cranberries.

Ingredients:

½ cup brown sugar

⅓ cup wheat-free flour

⅓ cup rolled oats

½ tsp. cinnamon

½ tsp. nutmeg

4 Tbsp. butter, softened

3 Granny Smith apples

2 pears

¼ cup dried sweetened cranberries

¼ cup water

Allergy Substitution Note:

In case of milk allergy, use non-dairy margarine in place of butter.

Directions:

1. Heat the oven to 375°F.

2. In a small mixing bowl, combine the brown sugar, flour, oats, cinnamon, and nutmeg.

3. Cut the butter into 8 or so pieces, and add them to the bowl. Use your fingertips to rub the butter into the sugar mixture until the topping is crumbly.

4. Core and then thinly slice the apples and pears. Layer the slices in an 8-inch-square baking pan. Top them with the dried sweetened cranberries.

5. Pour the water over the fruit. Then sprinkle on the crumb topping.

6. Bake the crisp until the fruit slices are tender, about 40 minutes. Serve it warm, either plain or topped with vanilla ice cream.

Goofy's Cinnamon Apples

(Serves 4)

Calories: 180   Total Fat: 3 grams   Total Carbohydrate: 39 grams   Fiber: 3 grams   Protein: 1 gram

Goofy is always inspired by his trips to the market, no matter what season it is! His signature dessert is safely cut with an apple slicer and easily simmered in 15 minutes.

Ingredients:

4 medium apples, peeled (McIntosh or Granny Smith work best)

½ cup light brown sugar

1 tsp. ground cinnamon

¼ tsp. ground nutmeg

4 Tbsp. water

1 Tbsp. butter

Allergy Substitution Note:
In case of milk allergy, use non-dairy margarine in place of butter.

Directions:

1. Slice apples with an apple slicer. In a medium bowl, toss together apples, light brown sugar, cinnamon, and nutmeg.

2. Put apple mixture, water, and butter into a medium-sized saucepan, and cook it over medium heat, stirring occasionally, until apples are tender, 14 to 16 minutes.

TIP If the glaze becomes too thick, thin it by adding a Tbsp. of water at a time until it is the right consistency.

Minnie's Polka-Dot Fruit Sundae

(Makes 1)

Calculated using 1 Tbsp. raspberries, 1 Tbsp. white chocolate chips, and ½ cup ice cream

Calories: 270   Total Fat: 13 grams   Total Carbohydrate: 25 grams   Fiber: 1 gram   Protein: 3 grams

Decorated with white chocolate–filled berries, this sweet ice cream treat is proof that Minnie's got the scoop on sweet desserts.

Directions:

1. Wash the raspberries with cold water. Lightly pat them dry with a paper towel.

2. Place a white chocolate chip with the tip pointing down into the hollow center of each berry.

3. Scoop some vanilla ice cream into a serving dish. Top the scoop with the berry polka dots, gently pressing them against the ice cream just until they stick in place. Enjoy!

Ingredients:

Several fresh raspberries

White chocolate chips chips (such as Vermont Nut Free Chocolates® white chocolate chips)

Vanilla ice cream

Allergy Substitution Note:

In case of milk allergy, use non-dairy ice cream and non-dairy chocolate chips.

Mickey's Peppermint Bark

(Serves 8 - Serving size: 2 oz.)

Calories: 320   Total Fat: 16 grams   Total Carbohydrate: 46 grams   Fiber: 0 grams   Protein: 0 grams

This classic dessert is knotted with crushed peppermint and marshmallows.

Ingredients:

1 lb. white chocolate chips (such as Vermont Nut Free Chocolates® white chocolate chips)

½ cup candy canes or starlight mints, crushed

½ cup mini marshmallows

Allergy Note:

Chocolate can contain hidden ingredients such as milk or nuts. Be sure to check the ingredients to make sure the chocolate you buy is allergen-free and made in a peanut-free environment.

Some marshmallows contain eggs. Check the ingredients in case of an egg allergy.

Directions:

1. Line a 9- by 13-inch baking pan with parchment paper or aluminum foil. Set aside.

2. Place the white chocolate in a bowl and microwave for 30 seconds. Remove the bowl, stir the chocolate with a spatula, and place it back in the microwave. Continue to microwave the chocolate in 30-second periods until it has all melted.

3. Pour the chocolate into the baking pan and smooth it out with the spatula. Quickly sprinkle on the candy cane pieces and marshmallows, and lightly press them into the chocolate. Let the bark harden for at least an hour at room temperature before breaking into pieces.

TIP It's easy to crush candy canes, even without a blender. Just add a few candy canes to a zip-top bag and crush them with a rolling pin.

Scout's Hot Chocolate and Marshmallows

(Serves 8 - Serving size: 1 cup)

Calculated for hot chocolate without marshmallow

Calories: 220   **Total Fat: 3 grams**   **Total Carbohydrate: 42 grams**   **Fiber: 3 grams**   **Protein: 10 grams**

Calculated for hot chocolate with 1 marshmallow

Calories: 280   **Total Fat: 3 grams**   **Total Carbohydrate: 56 grams**   **Fiber: 3 grams**   **Protein: 10 grams**

Ingredients:

For marshmallows

(makes 36 marshmallows)

2 Tbsp. (2 packets) gelatin

2 cups granulated sugar

¼ tsp. salt

2 tsp. vanilla extract

2 Tbsp. silver sprinkles

¾ cup confectioners' sugar

For cocoa:

1 qt. whole milk

⅓ cup unsweetened cocoa powder

½ cup sugar

3 crushed peppermint sticks

Pinch of salt

Allergy Substitution Note:

In case of milk allergy, use dairy-free milk.

Scout loves to share this warm drink with his friends on cold days!

Directions:

To make the marshmallows:

1. Add ½ cup cold water to a small bowl and sprinkle the gelatin mixture on top. Set it aside for 10 minutes. Line a 9- by 13-inch baking pan with cling wrap, then spray it liberally with cooking spray. Set pan aside.

2. Place the granulated sugar and ½ cup cold water into a large saucepan and stir over medium heat until dissolved. Add the gelatin and bring to a boil. Remove from heat, carefully pour the mixture into a large bowl, and let stand until partially cool.

3. Add the salt and vanilla extract, and beat with an electric mixer until mixture is soft and doubles in volume, about 10 to 15 minutes. Pour the mixture into the pan and smooth it into the corners with a

spatula sprayed with cooking oil. Set aside until it becomes firm, about 3 hours.

4. Flip the marshmallows over and remove the cling wrap. Dust the sprinkles on top and cut out with a small star-shaped cookie cutter sprayed with cooking spray. Dip the bottom and edges of each star in confectioners' sugar, and set aside.

To make the cocoa:

5. Heat the milk in a large saucepan over medium-low heat. Be careful not to let it boil. Add the remaining ingredients, stir to dissolve, and pour into 4 individual mugs. Top with 1 or 2 marshmallows.

Tips for Traveling with Severe Allergies

Before You Go

Choose a place with a kitchen. You can book a vacation home or apartment through Web sites like VRBO.com and Airbnb.com. If you'd rather go the hotel route, look for rooms with kitchenettes so you can cook your own meals.

Contact the airline. Some airlines may be more allergy-friendly than others, so do some research before you book your ticket. Search online for an airline's allergy policy and call them to inform them of your child's allergy and hear what your options are. Although some airlines are unwilling to make many accommodations, others offer to make an announcement to all passengers that someone with a severe allergy to peanuts (for example) is on board and ask people to refrain from eating any peanuts they may have brought. Some airlines allow flight attendants, upon request, to create a buffer zone of rows of seats around a peanut-allergic passenger where no peanuts are to be consumed. At least one advises that customers with peanut allergies book flights that leave early in the morning, since the planes are given a thorough cleaning at the end of the day. Once you've chosen an air carrier, mention your child's allergy as you make your reservation; this may allow you to pre-board in order to wipe down your seating area, or even, in some cases, lead to a change in the snack options served on your flight.

Notify the hotel. "Items used at the hotel might expose your child to hidden allergens," says Brian Schroer, M.D., a pediatric allergist at Cleveland Clinic Children's Hospital. For instance, the cleaning staff may use latex gloves, or a welcome basket may contain nuts. If you're heading to an all-inclusive resort, it's crucial to speak with the chef or food director.

Create an allergy info card. For international trips, use an online translator to put your child's allergy information into the local language of the country you'll be visiting, then hand out the cards to restaurant staff and others as needed to alert them to your child's allergen(s) and the risk of cross-contact.

Pack epinephrine. Make sure your epinephrine auto-injectors aren't expiring soon, and consider picking up an extra pair in case one gets lost or improperly stored during your travels. As for any other medications your child takes (for asthma or other conditions), if you're going to be gone long enough, you may need a prescription override from your insurance so you can stock up on the right amount of medicine to cover the length of your trip before you leave.

En Route

Bring your own food. Flight attendants try to be helpful, but oftentimes they don't have an ingredient list on hand to guarantee how a meal was prepared. The last thing you ever want is an in-flight emergency. Bring some of your own food in case of questionable meals or travel delays.

Have medicine accessible. Whether you're flying on a plane or road-tripping in a car, make sure your child's medicine is easily in reach. For air travel, be sure to pack two epinephrine auto-injectors (EAIs) in your carry-on with a letter from your physician. (While doctors say you typically won't encounter a problem at the security gate, play it safe by bringing a note.) Store the EAIs according to the instructions that come with them because heat or light may affect the medicine.

Give yourself the aisle seat. To help protect your child from other fliers' food choices, give him or her the window seat or the middle seat between parents.

Do a wipe-down. As soon as you board a plane, train, or bus, use disinfecting wipes on everything your child might expose him- or herself to, including the seat and headrest, tray table, seat belt, seat back pocket (check to make sure it doesn't contain any trashed food wrappers), and emergency instructions.

> Part of finding your family's "new normal" with severe allergies is getting out of the protective bubble of home and back out in the world—whether it's on a faraway adventure or just a train ride to Grandma's. These strategies can help ensure a smooth trip.

Mylan is the global leader in providing treatment for potentially life-threatening (severe) allergies, and Disney is the world's leader in family entertainment. Now Mylan and Disney have formed an alliance to create unique resources for families like yours.

Mylan and Disney Publishing Worldwide are collaborating on books for families living with severe allergies, including a children's storybook and a cookbook. Mylan and Disney have also joined forces to launch a new website, MyAllergyKingdom.com, with helpful features for your family, including recommendations, tips, and real-life stories from experts and parents.

Mylan is a global pharmaceutical company that has been leading the effort to educate families and schools about life-threatening allergies and the importance of being ready to respond in case anaphylaxis occurs. Mylan's expertise coupled with the magic of Disney storytelling can help you and your family effectively manage living with severe allergies.

Visit MyAllergyKingdom.com to learn more about the Mylan-Disney alliance and to find other helpful resources regarding severe allergies.

RECALDENT™ and Device are trademarks of Cadbury Enterprises Pte Ltd.
KAMUT® is a registered trademark of Kamut International Ltd.
Egg Beaters® is a registered trademark of ConAgra Foods, Inc.
Enjoy Life® is a registered trademark of Enjoy Life Foods.
Vermont Nut Free Chocolates® is a registered trademark of Vermont Nut Free Chocolates.

ISBN 978-1-4847-4382-9
FAC-03427-15261
First Edition, September 2015
10 9 8 7 6 5 4 3 2 1
Printed in USA
Visit www.disneybooks.com

Content of this book was developed by Disney and reviewed in consultation with Mylan Inc.
NON-2015-0190 MYLAN® IS A REGISTERED TRADEMARK OF MYLAN INC.

NOT FOR RESALE

Disclaimer: The content of this book is not intended as medical advice. Families should check with their healthcare professionals regarding the treatment of severe food allergies.

Looking for tips on severe food allergies?
Visit www.MyAllergyKingdom.com

AMERICAN IMPRESSIONISM
CALIFORNIA SCHOOL

FLEISCHER MUSEUM

THE PERIMETER CENTER

17207 North Perimeter Drive Scottsdale, Arizona 85255

FLEISCHER MUSEUM

17207 North Perimeter Drive
Scottsdale, Arizona 85255
(602) 585-3108

Designed and Produced by Bluefisch Productions
Phoenix, Arizona

AMERICAN IMPRESSIONISM CALIFORNIA SCHOOL

Selections from the permanent collection
and loans from the Paul and Kathleen Bagley collection.

Essays by Jean Stern

FLEISCHER MUSEUM

Forward by Donna H. Fleischer
Director, Fleischer Museum

The publication of this catalog represents a new era for the Fleischer Collection and this period of American Impressionism. For the past years as the collection evolved, it has been displayed in the Phoenix corporate headquarters of Franchise Finance Corporation Of America, a financial services institution founded in the spirit of democratic capitalism. Early in 1990, FFCA moved into its new 56,000 square foot facility at The Perimeter Center in Scottsdale. This two story headquarters, constructed of materials indigenous to Arizona, also houses the Fleischer Museum, the permanent home for the Fleischer Collection of American Impressionism, California School.

The Fleischer Museum is the first museum dedicated to this period of art. Although the California school was long overlooked as a regional school of American Impressionism, recent scholarship and definitive exhibitions have established it as an important and integral part of the history of American Art.

The artists who make up the permanent collection were formally trained, professional artists who traveled and painted internationally. At some point in their careers, they came to California with renewed spirits to paint in the out of doors. They fell in love with California and settled there for many reasons, none the least were the fine climate, the beauty of the diverse landscape, and the availability of bright, sunny days. Their enthusiasm for this environment is well documented by the extensive body of work painted by these American Impressionists. This group, who painted and exhibited together, included graphic artists, scenic painters, china painters, and mural painters as well as easel painters. Many of these painters worked in the French Impressionist style and all of them shared an abiding interest in landscape. However, they developed their own distinct style and as a school, they gained respect and renown for their descriptive interpretation of the light and land in California, throughout the United States as well as other parts of the world. In their organized pursuit of art, these artists formed the California Art Club in 1909 and the Laguna Beach Art Association in 1918. They enjoyed great critical and financial success for over three decades. It was not until the advent of modernism in the 1940's that these and many other American artists slipped into ill-deserved anonymity. The representational period was left behind as the popularity of modern art increased. Finally in the 1970's, interest in this period was renewed. Art historians, museums and galleries began researching this fascinating period and its personalities. The Fleischer Collection was a directive force that helped bring about this awareness. *Masterworks of California Impressionism,* a book on the FFCA, Morton H. Fleischer Collection, was published in 1986. It was distributed and sold nationwide. A landmark exhibition occurred in 1988 when the Fleischer Collection was exhibited at the Gilcrease Museum in Tulsa, Oklahoma. This was the first significant exhibition of this material outside of California.

Now the Fleischer Museum is dedicated to preserving these masterworks of art by giving these artists and this period of American Impressionism the recognition that it so richly deserves. Not only is the Fleischer Museum dedicated to their perpetuity but also to the continued education of all people who view this collection. My husband and I have shared many joyous moments together assembling and displaying this collection. It is with great pride that we present our collection for all to share in the beauty and joy that these artists so masterfully and wonderfully painted.

BISCHOFF, FRANZ A.

(1864-1929)

Bischoff was called the "King of the Rose Painters," and his unequaled reputation was founded in work in the difficult medium of porcelain painting as well as magnificent oil paintings such as ROSES, painted circa 1912.

Born and trained in Europe, Bischoff established himself as the premier china painter in America, a ranking which still applies today among collectors. In 1906, he settled in Southern California and began a "second career" as a painter of still-lifes and landscapes. His sociability and technical virtuosity as a painter endeared him to the California art community and his studio became a favorite meeting place for artists in Los Angeles.

Bischoff's paintings are remarkable for their brilliant use of color. In MOUNT ALICE AT SUNSET, painted circa 1920, Bischoff shows the craggy granite monolith in tones of pink, red and mauve, with occasional green highlights, next to white and blue snow, all superimposed on a mustard colored sky. In spite of these provocative and irritable colors, the scene perfectly captures the effect of a late afternoon glow in the High Sierras. Likewise his distinctive treatment of the banal and often repeated subject of the CAPISTRANO MISSION becomes a glorious celebration of bold color and vivid light.

Bischoff's strength and genius as a colorist carries his works from the bold Impressionism of his early period to a powerful and dramatic Post-Impressionism based on color and its essential role in art.

FRANZ A. BISCHOFF
ROSES
40″ x 50″ O/C

FRANZ A. BISCHOFF
MOUNT ALICE AT SUNSET
34″ x 30″ O/C

FRANZ ARTHUR BISCHOFF
CAPISTRANO MISSION
24″ x 30″ O/C
on loan from Paul and Kathleen Bagley

FRANZ ARTHUR BISCHOFF
MONTEREY CYPRESS
24″ x 30″ O/C
on loan from Paul and Kathleen Bagley

FRANZ ARTHUR BISCHOFF
CATHEDRAL POINTS, UTAH
30″ x 40″ O/C

BOTKE, JESSIE ARMS

(1883-1971)

The paintings of Jessie Arms Botke are a unique and wonder-filled world all their own. Most often, they are pictures of birds, a large variety including white peacocks, blue peacocks, cockatoos, ducks, swans, geese, pheasants, and toucans, among others. The birds are shown in natural settings accompanied by carefully painted flora, with studiously observed renditions of leaves and flowers. Far from being mere pictures of birds and plants, her paintings are richly adorned with an abundance of minutely rendered detail: every petal, every leaf and every feather becomes an important element of the whole pictorial scheme.

TWO PEACOCKS ON A GRAPEVINE shows the profusion of detail and elegant line which, when combined with the soft muted colors, make Botke's work a significant factor in the American Art Deco style. The decorative richness of this painting is enhanced by the addition of the gold-leaf background, a stylistic element borrowed from Medieval illuminated manuscripts.

WHITE PEACOCK, COCKATOOS AND FLOWERS by contrast, does not have the gold-leaf background, but instead relies on the overwhelming bounty of flowers to give the painting its sense of extravagance. It is estimated that there are close to fifty varieties of flowers in this *tour de force* of American painting.

JESSIE ARMS BOTKE
TWO PEACOCKS ON A GRAPEVINE
30″ x 25″ O & Gold LF/M

JESSIE ARMS BOTKE
WHITE PEACOCK , COCKATOOS AND FLOWERS
48″ x 64.75″ O/C

BRANDRIFF, GEORGE KENNEDY

(1890-1936)

George Brandriff was a practicing professional dentist in Southern California when he began to take art lessons in 1918. His passion for art eventually overtook him and in 1928 he closed his practice to become a full-time artist. In his short and tragic life, Brandriff proved to be one of the most moving and enigmatic figures of the California Impressionists.

Brandriff's works are generally painted in bold, colorful brushstrokes, often in powerful and daring compositions and suffused with a strong light. INTO THE SUNSET shows a group of mounted Indians receding into a deep canyon. The composition of this painting is very stark, with a brightly lit cliff face bordered by ominously shaded foreground and side. The combination of light and shade coming together at the point where the Indians meet gives this remarkable painting its feeling of finality. The sunset expressed by this painting is not merely the end of the day but rather the end of a way of life.

DRYING SAND uses the metaphorical image of the deserted beach with the purity of the air, ocean and sand, to convey an eerie feeling of loneliness and isolation. The powerful images evoked by Brandriff's paintings must surely reflect the deep uneasy spirituality of the artist, a man, who when confronted with the reality of his terminal cancer, chose to end his life by suicide.

GEORGE KENNEDY BRANDRIFF
INTO THE SUNSET, NEW MEXICO
30″ x 36″ O/C

GEORGE KENNEDY BRANDRIFF
DRYING SAND
24″ x 28″ O/C

BRAUN, MAURICE
(1877-1941)

Hungarian by birth, Maurice Braun came to the United States with his parents and settled in New York City in 1881. He studied painting for three years at the school of the National Academy and took an additional year with the celebrated American Impressionist William Merritt Chase. By 1909, Braun was an established portrait painter in New York. Feeling the need to expand his scope, Braun came to California and turned to landscape painting.

Braun established a studio and an art academy in San Diego. His affiliation to the Theosophical Society was surely a strong influence on his artistic development. That group's philosophy led Braun to take art as a subjective experience, not merely a visual pursuit. Many of his paintings represent nature as an entity that shows many different moods.

During the 1920s, Braun exhibited widely both in the East and West. He kept residences and studios in Silvermine, and Old Lyme, Connecticut, both of which were regional centers of American Impressionism. In 1929, he became one of the founders of the Contemporary Artists of San Diego and was considered the most important artist in San Diego.

PT. LOMA HILLSIDE shows the great similarity between Braun and the style of his mentor, William Merritt Chase. It is a work of sunlight and brilliance, capturing the flavor and feel of a breezy summer day in San Diego.

MAURICE BRAUN
POINT LOMA HILLSIDE
25″ x 30″ O/C

CLAPP, WILLIAM

(1879-1954)

Born in Canada and raised in Oakland, California, Clapp spent several years studying art in France in the early 1900s. In Paris, he fell under the influence of the Impressionist painters, especially Renoir, and later adopted a Neo-Impressionist style based on the works of Georges Pierre Seurat and Paul Signac. This style, generally termed "pointillism," relies on the effect of a multitude of dots of color to create a vibrant and radiant picture.

Clapp returned to Oakland in 1917 and began his friendship with a group of young artists who exhibited together as the "Society of Six." In 1918, Clapp became the curator of the Oakland Art Gallery, a post he held until 1949. In this capacity, he was instrumental in the success of the Society of Six as he instituted an annual exhibition program for them starting in 1923. The most conservative member of the Society of Six, Clapp remained a Neo-Impressionist all his life, where the other members experimented with Expressionsim and other Modernist styles during the 1920s and 1930s.

STEEP CITY STREET, 1944 was painted in Berkeley, California. It shows Clapp's characteristic pointillist style, with the entire surface of the painting covered with small daubs of color. From a distance, these dots of color blend with the surrounding dots to create a vivid, realistic sense of natural light.

WILLIAM CLAPP
STEEP CITY STREET, 1944
20″ x 24″ O/B

CLARK, ALSON SKINNER

(1876-1949)

One of the most diligent practitioners of Impressionism in America, Clark developed his style with four years of study under William Merritt Chase in New York, followed by a fateful year with James A. Whistler in Paris. Over his long and productive career, Clark won numerous awards including a Bronze Medal at the St. Louis Exposition, 1904, the Martin B. Cahn Prize at the Art Institute of Chicago, 1906, a Bronze Medal at the Panama Pacific International Exposition, 1915 and the Huntington Prize, Los Angeles Museum in 1924.

Clark's early paintings, such as SUNSET, NORMANDY, c. 1901, are greatly influenced by the works of James A. Whistler. They are essentially poetic paintings using soft, muted colors, combined for a gentle, harmonious effect. Often, these early works are posed from an oblique perspective, as in FROM OUR WINDOW, PARIS, 1903, painted in his Paris apartment. From about 1910-1911, Clark's work takes on a definite Impressionist palette and technique, partly due to his exposure to the style of Claude Monet on a seminal visit to Giverny. THOUSAND ISLANDS, painted c. 1911, shows this remarkable turn to Impressionism and the almost complete abandonment of Whistler's influence. The painting is covered with a brilliant pattern of color applied in a lively brushstroke.

ALSON SKINNER CLARK
THOUSAND ISLANDS
29.5″ x 37.5″ O/C

ALSON SKINNER CLARK
SUNSET, NORMANDY
25.5″ x 32″ O/C

ALSON SKINNER CLARK
FROM OUR WINDOW, PARIS 1903
25.25″ x 31.75″ O/C

ALSON SKINNER CLARK
FROZEN RIVER
25″ x 31″ O/B
on loan from Paul and Kathleen Bagley

COOPER, COLIN CAMPBELL

(1856-1937)

Cooper studied art with Thomas Eakins, the influential American realist who taught at the Pennsylvania Academy of the Fine Arts in Philadelphia. In 1886, he went to Europe, painting in Holland, Belgium and later in Paris. Returning to the United States in 1895, he became an instructor at the Drexel Institute in Philadelphia.

Cooper established a reputation as a painter of architectural subjects. He travelled widely in Europe, the Middle East and India producing magnificent paintings of important buildings. In America, he painted a series of urban views with newly emerging skyscrapers in New York, Philadelphia and Chicago.

By 1915, Cooper began to spend time in Los Angeles and San Diego and in 1921 he established a home and studio in Santa Barbara, where he lived and painted until his death in 1937. He was made a member of the National Academy in 1912 and won numerous prizes in his career, including a Gold Medal at the Panama-Pacific International Exposition in San Francisco in 1915.

A CALIFORNIA WATER GARDEN AT REDLANDS, CA. was painted at Kimberly Crest, the home of J.A. Kimberly, of the Kimberly-Clark Paper Company, in Redlands. Built in 1897, this French Chateau style mansion is now a museum. Cooper painted several works at Kimberly Crest in 1929. This example shows the house from the lily pond. It is painted in Cooper's elegant Impressionist style, full of light and color and covered with countless small brushstrokes.

COLIN CAMPBELL COOPER
A CALIFORNIA WATER GARDEN AT REDLANDS, CA.
29.5″ x 36.5″ O/C

FRANCISCO, JOHN BOND
(1863-1931)

The most notable figure of the arts in Los Angeles at the turn of the century, J. Bond Francisco was both the most famous painter and leading violinist of his day. After several years of study in Munich and Paris, Francisco came to Los Angeles in the late 1880s where he became a founding member of the Los Angeles Art Association. In 1897, he was a founding member of the Los Angeles Symphony Orchestra, serving as the first Concert Master.

Francisco's early works are fully in the European traditional style, reflecting his training in Munich. These are principally figural studies and realistic still-life subjects. His style evolved to a more impressionistic mode while still retaining the darker tonalities associated with Barbizon paintings. He became known for his brilliantly colored sunset scenes and bright, hazy desert paintings.

In 1906, Francisco was commissioned by the Santa Fe Railroad to paint several views of the Grand Canyon which were later used as advertisements for travel brochures. GRAND CANYON, painted on this occasion, was retained by the artist and handed down to his son. CALIFORNIA LANDSCAPE shows Francisco's virtuosity in handling the delicate light that is so characteristic of the Southern California foothills. Paintings of this monumental size were rarely produced, and then only for special exhibitions or commissions.

JOHN BOND FRANCISCO
CALIFORNIA LANDSCAPE
46″ x 64″ O/C

JOHN BOND FRANCISCO
GRAND CANYON
34″ x 46″ O/C

GAMBLE, JOHN
(1863-1957)

John Gamble was California's premier painter of wildflowers. His interest in wildflowers was not in the flowers themselves but rather in the colorful patterns they made upon the gentle rolling hills. The color of the orange-yellow poppies was so bold that some critics affectionately referred to his paintings as "Gamble's Prairie Fires."

Born in New Jersey, Gamble grew up in New Zealand and came to study art in San Francisco in 1883. In 1890, he embarked for Paris to study at the Academie Julian and the Academie Colarossi, and in 1893, came back to San Francisco to open his studio as a professional artist.

He quickly developed a reputation as a painter of wildflowers by following a yearly routine of travelling up and down California to portray the springtime spectacle. The long list of flowers that appear in his paintings include the California poppy, blue and yellow lupines, sage, wild lilacs, wild buckwheat, desert verbena, blue and white everlasting and owl's clover.

The San Francisco earthquake of April 18, 1906, nearly ruined Gamble. His studio and its entire contents were destroyed in the ensuing fire. Soon thereafter, Gamble left San Francisco to live in Los Angeles, at the urging of his close friend Elmer Wachtel. On his way to Los Angeles he passed through Santa Barbara and immediately fell in love with the small coastal community. He altered his plans and took up residence in Santa Barbara where he lived and painted for the rest of his life.

JOHN GAMBLE
POPPIES AND LUPINES (SANTA BARBARA)
18″ x 24″ O/C

JOHN GAMBLE
POPPIES AND YELLOW LUPINES, POINT LOBOS
20″ x 30″ O/C
on loan from Paul and Kathleen Bagley

GRAY, PERCY
(1869-1952)

Born in San Francisco, Percy Gray learned the art of painting at the California School of Design under the directorship of Emil Carlsen. He supported himself by working for a San Francisco newspaper as a staff artist. In 1895, he went to New York and studied under William Merritt Chase.

He returned to San Francisco in 1906, the year of the Great Earthquake. In 1915, he won the Bronze Medal for watercolor at the Panama-Pacific International Exposition in San Francisco and the First Prize for Watercolor at the Arizona Art Exhibition in Phoenix. Secure in his career as a watercolor painter, Gray opened a studio in San Francisco and over the years established himself as a sensitive artist of the California landscape. His work captures the soft, hazy atmosphere of the overcast Northern California morning. Very often, Gray's paintings are set in a gentle rolling meadow or below sloping hills. It may be a field of flowering California poppies set within a stand of elegant eucalyptus or rugged oak, with a deep space disappearing in the mist. It may also be a bleak coastal scene, with cold blues and grays hovering over jagged rock. At all times, however, Gray's paintings are tonal poems presented with gentle eloquence and great beauty.

In 1923, Gray married Leone Phelps and moved to Monterey. Gray became active in the thriving art community and exhibited regularly with the Carmel Art Association. In 1940, he won a painting prize at the Golden Gate International Exposition in San Francisco. Towards the end of his life, Gray found himself fighting the force of modernism, yet his beautiful paintings of the California land sold readily and he never changed his style.

PERCY GRAY
MEADOW WITH POPPIES
11.5″ x 15″ WC/P

HANSEN, ARMIN CARL
(1886-1957)

Armin Hansen was the son of the celebrated western painter Herman W. Hansen, and it was with his father that Armin first studied art. In 1903, he enrolled in the San Francisco Art Association's Mark Hopkins Institute of Art where he took classes under Arthur F. Mathews. He then spent the next several years in Europe, painting and studying in Germany and Belgium. He returned to San Francisco in 1912 and in 1916 he settled in the coastal village of Monterey.

A vigorous and powerful painter, Hansen's style is marked by bold and free brushwork, loose and painterly application of color and, at times, by daring compositional structure. His artistic approach made Hansen a popular and respected teacher in the San Francisco art community. In 1926, he was elected Associate of the National Academy and, in 1948, to full membership. His long list of awards include a Silver Medal at the Panama-Pacific International Exposition, 1915, First Hallgarten Prize at the National Academy, 1920, and the Ranger Purchase Prize, National Academy in 1925. Hansen was also a superb etcher and among the many awards in that medium was the Gold Medal in Paris, 1938.

RUNNING FREE, painted circa 1930, shows Hansen's remarkable style, painted with bold, free strokes of color. By placing the ship in an oblique position in the upper right corner of the painting, Hansen gives the viewer the dramatic feeling of the violent open sea.

ARMIN CARL HANSEN
RUNNING FREE
18″ x 22″ O/B

ARMIN CARL HANSEN
STILL LIFE WITH BOWLS
39″ x 33″ O/B
on loan from Paul and Kathleen Bagley

45

HARRIS, SAM HYDE
(1889-1977)

Sam Hyde Harris was a big man, with a forceful personality, full of warmth and openly charming. By contrast, his paintings are soft, gentle statements, colored in soft, poetic tones and exuding a deep spirituality and love of nature. He had a deep interest in the freshness of the early California morning with particular fondness for the effects of fog and haze.

ARROYO SECO is a view of the dry riverbed that runs from Pasadena to Los Angeles. Here, Harris paints the glistening light reflecting from the dew laden trees and bushes in the early morning haze. He creates the deep, misty distance by carefully adding white and blue to the receding hillside.

BLUE AND ORANGE was painted in Sunset Beach, a seaside town south of Los Angeles where Harris lived from 1931-1937. Harris was one of the very few artists who turned their attention to the urban environment. He found great beauty in the everyday settings of houses and streets of Southern California.

Born in England, Harris emigrated to America in 1904 and settled in Los Angeles. He spent most of his active career as a commercial artist for clients such as the Santa Fe Railroad, producing posters and brochures. He painted during the weekends or whenever he had time off and rarely sold any of his early period work. In his later years, he was very active in local art associations and came to be a respected leader and teacher.

SAM HYDE HARRIS
ARROYO SECO
25″ x 30″ O/C

SAM HYDE HARRIS
BLUE AND ORANGE
16″ x 20″ O/B
on loan from Paul and Kathleen Bagley

HILLS, ANNA ALTHEA
(1882-1930)

One of the founding members of the Laguna Beach Art Association, Anna Hills studied at the Art Institute of Chicago and the Cooper Union Art School in New York. She travelled widely in Europe, painting in England, France and Holland. Upon her return to the United States, she lived in Los Angeles briefly before moving to Laguna Beach in 1913.

Her dedicated and tireless efforts at organization made her a leader of the important Laguna Beach School, serving as president of the association from 1922 to 1925, and again from 1927 to 1930. Her community interests also led to several group exhibitions, lectures and a long career as a teacher in Laguna Beach.

Hills was a close friend and painting partner to several important California painters, including George Brandriff and Edgar Payne. Her distinctive style was essentially a bright Impressionistic approach, full of small patches of pure color, modified by the use of a small palette knife to flatten the surface. In THE OLD RANCH, she alters the horizon line and draws the viewer's attention to the brilliant effect of color and light on the surface of the pond in the foreground. The use of a large area of rippling water, with small patches of color reflecting the sky, trees and buildings, was a favorite device among the French Impressionists, and when successfully employed, added greatly to the overall brilliance of the work.

ANNA ALTHEA HILLS
OLD RANCH
24" x 20" O/C

KLEITSCH, JOSEPH
(1885-1931)

Born in Hungary, Joseph Kleitsch was an internationally successful portrait painter before coming to the United States sometime around 1914. He settled in Chicago where he continued to paint portraits as well as teach and exhibit at the Art Institute of Chicago, from 1914 to 1919.

In 1920, Kleitsch moved to Laguna Beach. Impressed by the natural beauty and idyllic charm of the small village, he began to paint views of Laguna Beach and landscapes of its environs. These paintings are noteworthy in capturing the various moods of the picturesque community and preserve with touching nostalgia a way of life which has passed with modern times.

From 1926 to 1929, Kleitsch toured Europe, staying in Paris and painting in Giverny, the small town where Claude Monet had made his home. He returned to his native Hungary and later, in 1929, painted in Spain.

Kleitsch's style is a unique approach to Impressionism with a freshness and fluidity of paint application. His landscapes are vivid and he captured the bright, clear light of the coast with acute facility. His views of Laguna Beach are realistic portrayals of the streets and houses, yet sometimes they are peopled with classically posed groups of passers-by as though in a curious stage-like setting. His portraits are truly remarkable for their life-like appearance and deeply emotive presence.

One of the stalwart members of the Laguna Beach Art Association, Kleitsch received numerous awards during his life for both his landscapes and figure paintings.

JOSEPH KLEITSCH
CARMEL CYPRESS (detail)
30″ x 26″ O/C

JOSEPH KLEITSCH
EVENING AT LAGUNA
16″ x 20″ O/C
on loan from Paul and Kathleen Bagley

LAURITZ, PAUL
(1889-1976)

Born and trained in Norway, Paul Lauritz spent a good part of his youth between odd jobs and occasional commercial art commissions. He eventually ended up in Alaska with the gold rush and it was there that he met the artist Sydney Laurence. His years as a gold miner were fruitless but the more valuable by-product was his association with Laurence who was instrumental in the young artist's development.

Discouraged with mining and determined to become a full-time artist, Lauritz came to Los Angeles in 1919 and opened a studio for portrait and decorative painting. Through the early 1920s, he made a living as a painter and teacher, holding classes at Chouinard Art Institute and at Otis Art Institute. He painted throughout California, the desert, the Sierras, and the coast in Carmel, Monterey and Laguna Beach. He was renown for his seascapes and landscapes with large, cloud-filled skies. Many of his paintings have a poetic, dream-like color tone, while others are bright and sun-filled.

In 1925, he returned to Norway and was commissioned by the king for a large seascape to hang in the palace. In 1928, he won the Purchase Prize at the San Diego Museum and in 1939, was awarded a Gold Medal in San Francisco.

END OF WINTER, HIGH SIERRAS is a monumental *tour de force* painted in a fully Impressionist style. The entire work is painted in small strokes of color, carefully applied in a pattern designed to approximate the natural fluidity and brilliance of light. From a distance, these dots blend with one-another to create the convincing effect of a warm spring day in the Sierras.

PAUL LAURITZ
END OF WINTER, HIGH SIERRAS
50″ x 60″ O/C

MITCHELL, ALFRED R.
(1888-1972)

Alfred Mitchell was born in York, Pennsylvania. As a boy, he dabbled in sculpture and painting but took no formal instruction until he turned twenty-five. In 1913, he began his studies with Maurice Braun in San Diego. One of the first paintings he exhibited, at the Panama-California Exposition in San Diego in 1915, earned him a Silver Medal. Spurred by his success, he enrolled in the Pennsylvania Academy in 1916, taking classes with Daniel Garber, Philip Hale and Joseph T. Pearson. In 1920, the academy awarded him the Cresson European Scholarship, a prestigious prize judged by competition.

Upon his return from Europe, Mitchell opened a studio in San Diego and initiated a long course of teaching and exhibition that made him one of the most respected artists in Southern California. In 1937, he won the Leisser-Farnham Prize at the San Diego Museum. He was a member of the Laguna Beach Art Association and received its Highest Award in 1940.

Mitchell's style evolved from an earlier Impressionist style, very much indebted to the Bucks County Impressionists and especially to Edward Redfield, who was a close friend of Mitchell. With time, Mitchell turned to a more realistic approach, somewhat reminiscent of Edward Hopper but with stronger and more dramatic color. SUMMER HILLS and AT THE VILLAGE INN both date from 1929 and are full of the vigor and brightness that characterizes Mitchell's fully mature Impressionist period.

ALFRED R. MITCHELL
SUMMER HILLS
40″ x 50″ O/C

ALFRED R. MITCHELL
AT THE VILLAGE INN, 1929
40″ x 50″ O/C
on loan from Paul and Kathleen Bagley

PAYNE, EDGAR ALWIN
(1882-1947)

Essentially self-taught, Edgar Payne spent several years as a house painter, sign painter, scenic artist and mural decorator before turning to full-time easel painting. In 1911, Payne visited California, staying in Laguna Beach and working his way up the coast to San Francisco, painting along the way. In San Francisco, he met the young artist Elsie Palmer whom he married the following year. In 1917, the two moved to Laguna Beach where Edgar Payne initiated and became the founding president of the Laguna Beach Art Association.

Payne painted throughout California, becoming well-known for his forceful paintings of the High Sierras and the rocky surf at Laguna. In 1922, he, Elsie and their daughter Evelyn went on a two-year trip to Europe, where they painted views of the Alps as well as the fishing fleet in Brittany and Venice. In 1923, he won an Honorable Mention for his view of Mont Blanc at the Paris Salon. Upon his return to America, Payne settled in Los Angeles, though he often visited Laguna and remained active in the Laguna Beach Art Association.

Payne is perhaps the best known of the California Impressionists. His distinctive style, with his large, painterly brushstrokes, coupled to his penchant for dramatic subject matter, makes his work uniquely recognizable. His book on structure and composition can be found in most artists' libraries and his many awards include the Cahn Prize in 1921 and the Ranger Prize in 1929.

EDGAR ALWIN PAYNE
BRITTANY SKY
34″ x 34″ O/C

63

EDGAR ALWIN PAYNE
HOME PORT
28″ x 34″ O/C
on loan from Paul and Kathleen Bagley

EDGAR ALWIN PAYNE
BLUE LAKE, CALIFORNIA
28″ x 34″ O/C

EDGAR ALWIN PAYNE
CHIOGGIA HARBOR
42″ x 42″ O/C

EDGAR ALWIN PAYNE
CANYON DE CHELLY
28″ x 34″ O/C

PUTHUFF, HANSON DUVALL
(1875-1972)

After a brief period of study at the University of Denver Art School in 1893, and a year at the Chicago Academy of Fine Arts, Hanson Puthuff established himself in Denver in 1894 as a commercial artist, producing signs and posters for an advertising firm. In 1903, he moved to Los Angeles and together with art writer Antony Anderson founded the Art Students League of Los Angeles.

During the next few years, Puthuff painted on his own time while continuing to work for commissions, including a set of dioramas for the Los Angeles Museum of Natural History. In 1926, he made the fateful decision to retire from commercial art and devote his energies to fine art. He travelled widely in California, painting rolling hills and canyons, as well as the High Sierras.

One of his first commissions after the decision to quit his commercial art career in 1926 was from the Santa Fe Railroad. Puthuff was hired to paint a series of views of the Grand Canyon which were to be used by the railroad for promotion and advertising. In March, 1927, a gala exhibition was held in the Santa Fe offices to show these magnificent works to the public. GRAND CANYON, a majestic painting of monumental proportions, remained for many years a part of the Santa Fe Railroad art collection prior to its acquisition by the Fleischer Museum.

HANSON DUVALL PUTHUFF
GRAND CANYON
72.25″ x 96.12″ O/C

REIFFEL, CHARLES
(1862-1942)

Charles Reiffel worked at various jobs for most of his youth before turning to art in his late thirties. After working in a lithography shop and painting posters for an advertising firm, he left for Europe where he pursued a brief term of study with Carl von Marr at the Munich Academy.

Returning to the United States with a large number of sketches from Europe and North Africa, Reiffel began to exhibit his work at various shows. His unique style, comprised of a linear, string-like application of strokes of color, made him appear "modern" and progressive among his fellow painters. Unfortunately, his association with modernism made it difficult to sell his paintings.

In 1912, Reiffel moved to Silvermine, Connecticut, a small village popular with artists. He helped found and served as the first president of the Silvermine Guild of Artists. By 1921, he had finally cut all ties with commercial art and became a full-time painter.

Reiffel moved to Southern California in 1927, locating his home and studio in San Diego. He was a member of the San Diego Art Guild, the Contemporary Artists of San Diego, the California Art Club and the Laguna Beach Art Association. His many awards include the Harrison Prize, Los Angeles Museum, 1926, the Art Guild Prize, San Diego Museum, 1926, and the Gold Medal, California Art Club, 1928.

CHARLES REIFFEL
SNOWBOUND
34″ x 37″ O/C
on loan from Paul and Kathleen Bagley

RIDER, ARTHUR GROVER
(1886-1976)

Few painters have ever captured the true, overpowering intensity of sunlight as well as Arthur G. Rider. His work instantly brings to mind that of the powerful Spanish Impressionist Joaquin Sorolla. As an American Impressionist, Rider stands without comparison as the ultimate practitioner of Impressionist color theory.

Born in Chicago, Rider studied at the Chicago Academy of Fine Arts, followed by several years in Europe. While in Spain he met Sorolla, who became the greatest influence in his style. He returned to Valencia for several summers and in 1923, served as an honorary pallbearer at Sorolla's funeral.

In the late 1920's, Rider came to Southern California to paint in San Juan Capistrano and Laguna Beach. Favorably impressed by the climate and light of Laguna Beach, Rider purchased a house there in 1931. For more than thirty years he worked as a scenic artist for Twentieth Century Fox and Metro Goldwyn Mayer studios.

Rider's style is firmly founded on effective use of color. By applying complementary colors simultaneously, purple next to yellow, green next to red, Rider enhances the inherent brightness of these colors to produce the convincing effect of intense, natural sunlight. This is the essence of Impressionist color theory and when properly applied, the results are remarkable.

ARTHUR GROVER RIDER
SPANISH BOATS, c. 1922
40″ x 44″ O/C

ARTHUR GROVER RIDER
NEWPORT, WEST COAST
22″ x 23″ O/PNL

ARTHUR GROVER RIDER
FLOWERS, CAPISTRANO MISSION
28″ x 24″ O/C
on loan from Paul and Kathleen Bagley

ROSE, GUY
(1867-1925)

The scion of a wealthy landowning family, Guy Rose was born in the Los Angeles suburb of San Gabriel. He began his art studies at the California School of Design in San Francisco under Emil Carlsen. In 1888, he went to Paris where he studied for three years under Benjamin Constant, Lucien Doucet and Jules Lefebvre. He returned to America and lived and worked in New York as an illustrator for Harper's Magazine.

Rose was plagued throughout his life by a susceptibility to lead poisoning, a serious predicament since many oil paints of the day were based on lead white. Thus for the greater part of his life and the peak of his career, he was unable to paint in oils. It is a tragic irony that Rose, generally recognized as one of the best of the American Impressionists, was also the least prolific and his works are very scarce.

From 1904 to 1912, Rose and his wife Ethel, also a successful artist, lived as neighbors to Claude Monet in the little village of Giverny. Rose's friendship with Monet is clearly seen in the striking similarity of each artist's work. Rose also adopted Monet's method of painting a series of paintings of the same scene, each set at a slightly different time of day.

In 1912, Rose returned to New York and in 1914 came back to live in Los Angeles. He painted SAN GABRIEL MISSION soon after his return. Between 1914 and about 1921, when he suffered a stroke which left him unable to paint, he travelled throughout California. LAGUNA ROCKS, LOW TIDE dates from about 1916, while MIST OVER POINT LOBOS, one of a series of the Carmel-Monterey area, was painted about 1918.

GUY ROSE
MIST OVER POINT LOBOS
28.5″ x 24″ O/C

GUY ROSE
LAGUNA ROCKS, LOW TIDE
21″ x 24″ O/C
on loan from Paul and Kathleen Bagley

GUY ROSE
SAN GABRIEL MISSION
28.75″ x 23.75″ O/C

SCHUSTER, DONNA NORINE
(1883-1953)

Born in Milwaukee, Donna Schuster studied at the Art Institute of Chicago and at the Boston Museum School with Edmund C. Tarbell and Frank W. Benson. In the summer of 1912, she studied in Europe on a tour with William Merritt Chase.

In 1913, she took up residence in Los Angeles. The next year she took the Carmel summer class with William Merritt Chase and stayed in San Francisco to paint the construction of the buildings for the Panama-Pacific International Exposition which opened in 1915. She maintained a studio in Laguna Beach and was active in the Laguna Beach Art Association.

Schuster's career is marked by a succession of styles. Her training in Boston and her admiration of Tarbell were very influential in her early years, and many of her paintings have the distinctive "Boston" look. IN THE GARDEN, painted in 1917, is characteristic of her mature American Impressionist period and owes a great debt to the work of William Merritt Chase.

In the 1920s, Schuster constructed a lily pond in her back yard in tribute to Claude Monet. TIGER LILIES is one of a small series of lily paintings that relate to a brief flirtation with French Impressionism. In the late 1920s, she studied with the modernist Stanton Macdonald-Wright and her work of the period has a cubist-like tendency. Later, she experimented with Expressionism and other contemporary art movements.

Her prizes include a Silver Medal for watercolor at the Panama-Pacific International Exposition, 1915, and a First Prize, California Art Club, 1921.

DONNA NORINE SCHUSTER
IN THE GARDEN, 1917
30″ x 30″ O/C

DONNA NORINE SCHUSTER
TIGER LILIES
30″ x 30″ O/C

SMITH, JOHN CHRISTOPHER
(1891-1943)

J. Christopher Smith was born in Ireland and emigrated to America with his family sometime around 1903. He studied in New York with Robert Henri, the leading figure in the Ash Can School and a proponent of painting the activities of everyday American life.

In 1920, Smith came to Los Angeles. Many of his paintings show the plazas, streets and buildings of the city, with crowds of people milling about. In the mid 1920s, Smith made the acquaintance of Franz A. Bischoff and the two artists became close friends. Together they painted along the coast in Northern California, stopping in Monterey, Carmel and Cambria. Smith's painting of CAMBRIA shows his unique approach to color as a very bold and powerful statement. The houses are painted in a blaze of light giving the painting a feeling of very hot light and cool shade.

In 1928, Bischoff and Smith travelled to Utah to paint the sandstone cliffs of Zion National Park. In MT. MAJESTIC, ZION CANYON, Smith presents the cliffs emerging from a powerful and dramatic light, with great intensity between the dark and light areas of the painting.

After Bischoff's death in 1929, Smith retired from painting and turned his interests to interior design. He died of tuberculosis in 1943 at the age of fifty-two.

JOHN CHRISTOPHER SMITH
CAMBRIA, CALIFORNIA
24" x 30" O/C

JOHN CHRISTOPHER SMITH
MT. MAJESTIC, ZION CANYON
30″ x 40″ O/C

JOHN CHRISTOPHER SMITH
IRIS
30″ x 40″ O/C

SYMONS, GEORGE GARDNER

(1862-1930)

George Gardner Symons was a nationally known artist specializing in winter scenes of New England. He was also one of the first artists to discover Laguna Beach and he kept a home and studio there for over twenty years.

Born in Chicago, Symons was initiated into art at the Art Institute of Chicago before travelling to Paris, London and Munich for further study. Upon his return, he worked as a commercial artist while he painted in his spare time with his friend and fellow artist William Wendt. After a brief visit to California in the early 1880s, Symons persuaded Wendt to accompany him to Laguna Beach in 1896. In 1898, the two friends visited England and in 1903, Symons returned to Laguna Beach to become an active member of the art community. For a long time, Symons kept a studio in New York City and another in the Berkshires as well as the one in Laguna Beach.

In 1909, Symons won the Carnegie Prize at the National Academy. The Evans Prize came to him in 1910 and in 1911 he was elected to membership in the National Academy. In 1914, he was commissioned by the Santa Fe Railroad to paint several views of the Grand Canyon to be used in advertising and promotion. GRAND CANYON, a view of the gorge taken from a novel vantage point, is from this group.

Symons' style is solidly Impressionist accentuated by a realistic effect of shimmering light. His snowscenes are covered with areas of brilliant white flanked by deep and lively shade. His Laguna scenes are typically rocky shorelines with radiant spans of ocean, portrayed in lively masses of multi-colored brushstrokes.

GEORGE GARDNER SYMONS
GRAND CANYON
47″ x 70.5″ O/C

GEORGE GARDNER SYMONS
CONNECTICUT SNOW SCENE
25″ x 30″ O/C

GEORGE GARDNER SYMONS
WINTER STREAM
25″ x 30″ O/C
on loan from Paul and Kathleen Bagley

von SCHNEIDAU, CHRISTIAN
(1893-1976)

Christian von Schneidau was born in Sweden to a family of noble rank. A precocious child, he was given private art lessons and later enrolled at the Royal Academy of Fine Arts in Stockholm. In 1906, the family came to the United States and settled in Minnesota.

In 1910, von Schneidau won a scholarship to the Art Institute of Chicago, where he studied with Karl Albert Buehr and Wellington J. Reynolds. He excelled in drawing and figure work. In 1916, he won the John Quincy Adams Foreign Traveling Scholarship but could not go to Europe because of World War I. Instead, he toured the east coast.

An excellent portrait painter, von Schneidau moved to Los Angeles in 1917 to open a portrait studio. He quickly developed a good reputation and won commissions from many of Southern California's social elite. In 1920, von Schneidau took six months off and painted in Provincetown, Massachusetts, taking classes with Charles Webster Hawthorne, George Elmer Browne and Richard Miller, whose dynamic color contrasts greatly influenced von Schneidau's work.

For many years, von Schneidau was a portrait painter for Twentieth Century Fox, producing portraits of movie stars including Mary Pickford, Mary Philbin and Betty Grable. He also painted several murals, some of which are in the Forum Theater, the California Lutheran Hospital and the Chicago Swedish Club.

CHRISTIAN von SCHNEIDAU
PREENING
60″ x 45″ O/C

CHRISTIAN von SCHNEIDAU
FISH MARKET, PROVINCETOWN
46″ x 56″ O/C

CHRISTIAN von SCHNEIDAU
POINSETTIAS
36″ x 30″ O/C

WACHTEL, ELMER
(1864-1929)

Elmer Wachtel was one of the first professional artists to live in Los Angeles, arriving in 1882, three years before the completion of the Santa Fe Railroad's Chicago route which would precipitate the first great Los Angeles land boom. To supplement his meager income from painting, Wachtel also played violin in various orchestras.

Sometime about 1894, Wachtel moved to New York and briefly studied at the Art Students League with William Merritt Chase. He returned to California in 1896, staying with William Keith in San Francisco before coming home to Los Angeles. In 1903, he met Marion Kavanagh, a young artist who had been studying with Keith, and married her the next year. Together they spent more than twenty-five years travelling and painting together.

In 1929, Elmer Wachtel died while on a painting trip in Guadalajara, Mexico. Wachtel's style evolved from a traditional approach, based on the works of the French Barbizon painters, such as Diaz de la Peña and Theodore Rousseau. These earlier paintings are often dark and somber, with a small area of clear sky in the center of the painting. With time, Wachtel became influenced by Impressionism and used a lighter, more colorful palette, and a somewhat freer brush. He continued, however, to rely on tightly defined forms and solid draftsmanship.

ELMER WACHTEL
CALIFORNIA POPPIES
17" x 24" O/C

ELMER WACHTEL
CAPISTRANO MISSION
15″ x 25.5″ O/C

WACHTEL, MARION K.
(1876-1954)

Generally regarded as one of California's best artists, Marion Wachtel established her fame in watercolor painting, a difficult and unforgiving medium. Although the transparency of the paints allows for exquisite luminosity when handled properly, it does not permit correction or alteration of even the slightest error.

Born in Milwaukee, Marion Kavanagh was a promising member of an artistic family. She studied at the Art Institute of Chicago and in New York with William Merritt Chase. She taught painting at the Art Institute of Chicago prior to coming west to paint with William Keith in San Francisco.

In 1903, Keith suggested she visit Elmer Wachtel in Los Angeles to continue her studies. The two artists fell in love and were married the following year. Together they became an important aspect of the emerging Los Angeles art community and painted side by side until Elmer's death in 1929.

Marion Wachtel was an active exhibitor at the California Watercolor Society and the New York Aquarelists, to which she was elected member in 1922. It is said that Marion Wachtel refrained from painting in oil for fear that her work would eclipse that of Elmer's. After his death, she turned to oils but these paintings do not match the quality of her watercolors.

Wachtel's watercolors are noted for the unique representation of the California light, often set in the early morning, as in CHERRY VALLEY, CALIFORNIA, or in the late afternoon, with long, soft shadows contrasting the golden light of evening. Her paintings are carefully observed and realistic portraits of the land, yet they appear to be casual exercises, with a relaxed and unhurried feel.

MARION K. WACHTEL
CHERRY VALLEY, CALIFORNIA
20″ x 26″ WC/P
on loan from Paul and Kathleen Bagley

WARSHAWSKY, ABRAHAM G. (ABEL)
(1883-1962)

Abel Warshawsky grew up in Cleveland and studied art at the Cleveland School of Art with Louis Rorimer. In 1904, he was in New York studying at the National Academy of Design and the Art Students League.

In 1908, Warshawsky went to Paris where he developed his straightforward Impressionist style. Active in the Parisian art community, Warshawsky kept a studio in Paris for thirty years. He maintained a routine of travelling through France and Italy punctuated by annual trips to the United States to exhibit and sell his paintings.

In 1938, the impending outbreak of World War II compelled Warshawsky to return to America. He settled in Monterey where he built a studio, did portrait work and taught classes. He specialized in figural compositions often combined with the rugged coastline of Northern California. He was active in the Carmel Art Association, serving as president for one term.

GIRL IN GREEN was painted in France and shows Warshawsky's fully mature Impressionist style. The figure is carefully observed. Although the girl is posed in foreground shade, the soft light and incidental highlights reflected from her coat and blouse give her face a realistic sense of form. The background is handled in short and quick brushstrokes with abundant use of yellow highlight and purple shade.

ABRAHAM G. (ABEL) WARSHAWSKY
GIRL IN GREEN
32″ x 28″ O/C

WENDT, WILLIAM
(1865-1946)

William Wendt was one of America's preeminent landscape painters. Born in Germany, he came to the United States in 1880 and briefly studied at the Art Institute of Chicago. Otherwise, Wendt was essentially self-taught. In 1896, he visited California with his friend George Gardner Symons. In 1898, the two artists travelled to Cornwall, England. Finally, in 1906, Wendt and his wife, the sculptor Julia Bracken Wendt, settled in Los Angeles.

Wendt was a highly sensitive and spiritual individual. His great love of nature is evident in his paintings, almost always verdant landscapes untouched and unpopulated by man. He stood in awe of God's creations and often titled his paintings with passages from the Bible, such as I LIFTED MINE EYES UNTO THE HILLS, yet his works never show any outward signs of religious zeal and he advised against the conflicts of various creeds and sects. Wendt's spirituality was universal and open to all who viewed his paintings.

His early paintings show a combination of Realism and Impressionism, with a well developed sense of space. I LIFTED MINE EYES UNTO THE HILLS, winner of the Spalding Prize in 1922, has a tremendous sense of depth and atmosphere. In later paintings, Wendt concentrated on compositional form and surface treatment. Those works, such as SERENITY, painted in 1934, are much flatter in appearance with more attention to pattern and form than to realism. In his mature style, Wendt adopted a distinctive block-like application of paint which makes his work instantly recognizable.

WILLIAM WENDT
HOME OF THE QUAIL ,1928
24″ x 32″ O/C

WILLIAM WENDT
SERENITY
30″ x 36″ O/C
on loan from Paul and Kathleen Bagley

WILLIAM WENDT
I LIFTED MINE EYES UNTO THE HILLS
36″ x 50″ O/C

FLEISCHER MUSEUM
COLLECTION

Works included in the catalog are indicated
by page number.

Dana Bartlett
THE SYCAMORE
20″ x 24″ O/C

Louis Betts
UNTITLED—(PORTRAIT OF
GIRL WITH FLOWERS IN
GREEN CHAIR)
50″ x 37″ O/C

Franz A. Bischoff
A SUMMER'S PARTING
30″ x 34″ O/C

Franz A. Bischoff
PINNACLE ROCK, UTAH, 1928
30″ x 40″ O/C

Franz A. Bischoff
JAPANESE FISHING BOATS
19″ x 26″ O & WAX/B

Franz A. Bischoff
ARROYO SECO
12″ x 15″ O/B

Franz A. Bischoff
ROSES
40″ x 50″ O/C   Pg. 7

Franz A. Bischoff
WOMAN AT FOUNTAIN
6.75″ x 10″ O/C/B

Franz A. Bischoff
VALLEY LANDSCAPE
7″ x 10″ O/C/B

Franz A. Bischoff
ROSES (VASE)
6″ x 15.50″ PORCELAIN

Franz A. Bischoff
MOUNT ALICE AT SUNSET
34″ x 30″ O/C   Pg. 8

Franz A. Bischoff
RED MOUNTAIN
9.63″ x 13″ O/B

Franz A. Bischoff
CAPISTRANO MISSION
24″ x 30″ O/C   Pg. 9
On loan from Paul and Kathleen Bagley

Franz A. Bischoff
MONTEREY CYPRESS
24″ x 30″ O/C   Pg. 10
On loan from Paul and Kathleen Bagley

Franz A. Bischoff
CATHEDRAL POINTS, UTAH
30″ x 40″ O/C   Pg.11

Jessie Arms Botke
THREE DUCKS AT POND
8″ x 10″ O/P

Jessie Arms Botke
AVIARY, SAN DIEGO ZOO
18″ x 15″ WC/P

Jessie Arms Botke
TWO PEACOCKS ON A
GRAPE VINE
30″ x 25″ O & GOLD LF/M Pg. 13

Jessie Arms Botke
BUTTERFLIES & BIRDS (PAIR)
14″ x 12″ O/B

Jessie Arms Botke
SULPHUR CRESTED
COCKATOOS
7.25″ x 5.38″ O/B

Jessie Arms Botke
SALMON CRESTED
COCKATOOS
7″ x 6″ O/B

Jessie Arms Botke
WHITE PEACOCK, COCKATOOS
AND FLOWERS
48″ x 64.75″ O/C   Pg. 15

George Kennedy Brandriff
STEADY AS SHE BLOWS
20″ x 24″ O/C

George Kennedy Brandriff
INTO THE SUNSET, NEW MEXICO
30″ x 36″ O/C   Pg. 17

George Kennedy Brandriff
DRYING SAND
24″ x 28″ O/C   Pg. 19

George Kennedy Brandriff
PLAYING CARDS
24″ x 28″ O/C

Maurice Braun
POINT LOMA HILLSIDE
25″ x 30″ O/C   Pg. 21

Benjamin Chambers Brown
VALLEY OF LUPINE
25″ x 30″ O/C

William Clapp
BEACH SCENE
16″ x 20″ WAX/B

William Clapp
STEEP CITY STREET, 1944
20″ x 24″ O/B   Pg. 23

Alson Skinner Clark
THOUSAND ISLANDS
29.50″ x 37.50″ O/C   Pg. 25

Alson Skinner Clark
RAIL LINE PANAMA
25.50″ x 31.50″ O/C

Alson Skinner Clark
AUTUMN IN THE HILLS
15″ x 18″ O/C

Alson Skinner Clark
THE PATIO, MEXICO CITY
7.50″ x 9.50″ O/C/B

Alson Skinner Clark
SAN JUAN HARBOR,
PUERTO RICO
7.50″ x 9.50″ O/PNL

Alson Skinner Clark
SHORE NEAR LAGUNA BEACH
7.50″ x 9.50″ O/B

Alson Skinner Clark
STREET IN PANAMA
9.50″ x 7.50″ O/B

Alson Skinner Clark
THE STROLLERS
18″ x 15″ O/C

Alson Skinner Clark
SUNSET, NORMANDY
25.50″ x 32″ O/C   Pg. 27

Alson Skinner Clark
PUERTO RICAN HOUSES
7.50″ x 9.50″ O/B

Alson Skinner Clark
VIEW OF ANCON, PANAMA
25.50″ x 31.50″ O/C

Alson Skinner Clark
FROM OUR WINDOW, PARIS
1903
25.25″ x 31.75″ O/C   Pg. 28

Alson Skinner Clark
FROZEN RIVER
25″ x 31″ O/B   Pg. 29
On loan from Paul and Kathleen Bagley

Colin Campbell Cooper
A CALIFORNIA WATER
GARDEN AT REDLANDS, CA
(KIMBERLY CREST)
29.50″ x 36.50″ O/C   Pg. 31

Paul De Longpré
ROSES WITH HUMMINGBIRD
& BUMBLEBEE
20.75″ x 14.50″ WC/P

Paul I. Dougherty
ARIZONA SAGUARO
36″ x 34″ O/M

Raoul M. De Longpré Fils
BOUQUET OF YELLOW ROSES
AND LILACS
19″ x 26″ WC/P

Albert Fleury
PANORAMA OF THE GRAND
CANYON FROM EL TOVAR,
ARIZONA
30.12″ x 54.50″ O/C

Victor Clyde Forsythe
MORNING
25″ x 30″ O/C

John Bond Francisco
CALIFORNIA LANDSCAPE
46″ x 64″ O/C   Pg. 33

John Bond Francisco
GRAND CANYON
34″ x 46″ O/C   Pg. 35

John Bond Francisco
LANDSCAPE AT SUNSET
19″ x 24″ O/C

Charles Arthur Fries
CUYAMACA MOUNTAIN,
MIDDAY
16″ x 24″ O/C

John Gamble
CALIFORNIA LANDSCAPE
7.50″ x 13″ O/B

John Gamble
POPPIES AND LUPINES
(SANTA BARBARA)
18″ x 24″ O/C   Pg. 37

John Gamble
POPPIES AND YELLOW
LUPINES, POINT LOBOS
20″ x 30″ O/C   Pg. 39
On loan from Paul and Kathleen Bagley

Seldon C. Gile
GYPSY TRAIN
11.50″ x 16″ O/B

Percy Gray
MEADOW WITH POPPIES
11.50″ x 15″ WC/P   Pg. 41

Armin Carl Hansen
RUNNING FREE
18″ x 22″ O/B   Pg. 43

Armin Carl Hansen
SPRINGTIME IN THE GARDEN
10″ x 13″ O/B

Armin Carl Hansen
THE BROKEN CINCH
18″ x 24″ O/B

Armin Carl Hansen
STILL LIFE WITH BOWLS
39″ x 33″ O/B   Pg. 45
On loan from Paul and Kathleen Bagley

Sam Hyde Harris
ARROYO SECO
25″ x 30″ O/C   Pg. 47

Sam Hyde Harris
NEGLECTED
25″ x 30″ O/C

Sam Hyde Harris
DESERT (UNTITLED)
30″ x 44″ O/C

Sam Hyde Harris
SAN FERNANDO VALLEY
18″ x 24″ O/B

Sam Hyde Harris
BLUE AND ORANGE
16″ x 20″ O/B   Pg. 49
On loan from Paul & Kathleen Bagley

Thomas Hill
FALLS IN THE SIERRAS
30″ x 20″ O/C

Thomas Hill
WOODLAND GLADE WITH
TWO SQUIRRELS
50″ x 40″ O/C

Thomas Hill
VIEW OF YOSEMITE
53″ x 35″ O/C

Anna Althea Hills
MONTEZUMA'S HEAD
10″ x 14″ O/B

Anna Althea Hills
A HEAVY SURF
14″ x 18″ O/B

Anna Althea Hills
RADIANT SPRING
20″ x 24″ O/C

Anna Althea Hills
OLD RANCH
24″ x 20″ O/C   Pg. 51

Clarence Keiser Hinkle
YELLOW ROSES
11.50″ x 13.75″ O/B

Clarence Keiser Hinkle
ROCKPORT HARBOR
18″ x 22″ O/C

Clark Hobart
BETWEEN SHOWERS,
MONTEREY
24″ x 30″ O/C

Thomas L. Hunt
NEWPORT HARBOR
28″ x 30″ O/C

William L. Judson
MONTEREY LIVE OAKS
15″ x 25″ O/C

Joseph Kleitsch
CARMEL CYPRESS
30″ x 26″ O/C   Pg. 53

Joseph Kleitsch
EVENING AT LAGUNA
16″ x 20″ O/C   Pg. 55
On loan from Paul and Kathleen Bagley

Charles Krauth
SUNSHINE AND SHADOW,
ENCINITAS, CA
29″ x 33.75″ O/C

Paul Lauritz
END OF WINTER,
HIGH SIERRAS
50″ x 60″ O/C   Pg. 57

Jean Mannheim
LAGUNA VISTA
20″ x 24″ O/C

Jean Mannheim
LITTLE JEANNIE
17″ x 20″ O/C

Thomas Arnold McGlynn
WINDSWEPT CYPRESSES
25″ x 30″ O/C

Thomas Arnold McGlynn
THE SOUTHLAND
24.25″ x 28.25″ O/C

Alonso Megargee
GRAND CANYON
67″ x 47″ O/C

Alonso Megargee
INDIANS AT THE CANYON
40″ x 50.75″ O/C

Alonso Megargee
PETRIFIED FOREST
68.75″ x 47.25″ O/C

Alfred R. Mitchell
SUMMER HILLS
40″ x 50″ O/C   Pg. 59

Alfred R. Mitchell
BUCKS COUNTY IN THE
SNOW (PA)
16″ x 20″ O/B

Alfred R. Mitchell
SAN DIEGO MOUNTAINS
16″ x 20″ O/B

Alfred R. Mitchell
WISTERIA
9″ x 12″ O/B

Alfred R. Mitchell
AT THE VILLAGE INN, 1929
40″ x 50″ O/C   Pg. 61
On loan from Mr. and Mrs. Paul Bagley

De Witt Parshall
EUCALYPTUS AND FOG
24″ x 30″ O/PNL

Edgar Alwin Payne
BRITTANY SKY
34″ x 34″ O/C   Pg. 63

Edgar Alwin Payne
HOME PORT
28″ x 34″ O/C   Pg. 64
On loan from Paul and Kathleen Bagley

Edgar Alwin Payne
BLUE LAKE, CALIFORNIA
28″ x 34″ O/C   Pg. 65

Edgar Alwin Payne
SWISS VILLAGE
13″ x 16″ O/C/B

Edgar Alwin Payne
AUTUMN SYCAMORE
20″ x 24″ O/C

Edgar Alwin Payne
CHIOGGIA HARBOR
42″ x 42″ O/C   Pg. 66

Edgar Alwin Payne
OWENS VALLEY
10″ x 12″ O/B

Edgar Alwin Payne
MEDITERRANEAN BOAT
12.50″ x 15.50″ O/C/B

Edgar Alwin Payne
SWISS MT.
62″ x 62″ O/C

Edgar Alwin Payne
INDIANS ON HORSEBACK IN
SAGEBRUSH
40″ x 50″ O/C

Edgar Alwin Payne
EVENING GLOW
29″ x 29″ O/C

Edgar Alwin Payne
CANYON DE CHELLY
12″ x 15″ O/C/B

Edgar Alwin Payne
CANYON DE CHELLY
28″ x 34″ O/C   Pg. 67

Edgar Alwin Payne
ITALIAN BOAT & HOUSES,
CHIOGGIA
20″ x 25″ O/C

Edgar Alwin Payne
SARDINE BOATS
20″ x 24″ O/C

Edgar Alwin Payne
MT. TAMARACK
28″ x 34″ O/C

Edgar Alwin Payne
INDIAN BOY
11.05″ x 5″ O/B

Edgar Alwin Payne
PEAK OF ARGENTIERS
29.25″ x 29″ O/C

Edgar Alwin Payne
STAR OF INDIA
36″ x 45″ O/C

Edgar Alwin Payne
CANYON DE CHELLY
28″ x 34″ O/C

Edgar Alwin Payne
DESERT SKIES, NAVAJOS
25″ x 30″ O/C

Hanson Duvall Puthuff
EVENING—GRAND CANYON
12″ x 16″ O/B

Hanson Duvall Puthuff
JOYOUS SPRINGTIME
26″ x 30″ O/C

Hanson Duvall Puthuff
THE DESERT RAMPARTS—
ARIZONA
24″ x 30″ O/C

Hanson Duvall Puthuff
GRAND CANYON FROM
MAICORA POINT
60.25″ x 72.50″ O/C

Hanson Duvall Puthuff
GRAND CANYON
72.25″ x 96.12″ O/C   Pg. 69

Joseph Raphael
BURNING LEAVES
20″ x 26″ O/C

Granville S. Redmond
BEACH NEAR LA JOLLA
12″ x 16″ O/B

Charles Reiffel
IN THE BANNER VALLEY
34″ x 37″ O/C

Charles Reiffel
SNOWBOUND
34″ x 37″ O/C   Pg. 71
On loan from Paul and Kathleen Bagley

Arthur Grover Rider
MISSION FLOWERS,
CAPISTRANO
12.50″ x 16″ O/B

Arthur Grover Rider
SPANISH BOATS, c. 1922
40″ x 44″ O/C   Pg. 73

Arthur Grover Rider
NEWPORT, WEST COAST
22″ x 23″ O/PNL   Pg. 74

Arthur Grover Rider
FLOWERS, CAPISTRANO
MISSION
28″ x 24″ O/C   Pg. 75
On loan from Paul and Kathleen Bagley

Guy Rose
MIST OVER POINT LOBOS
28.50″ x 24″ O/C   Pg. 77

Guy Rose
LAGUNA ROCKS, LOW TIDE
21″ x 24″ O/C   Pg. 78
On loan from Paul & Kathleen Bagley

Guy Rose
SAN GABRIEL MISSION
28.75″ x 23.75″ O/C   Pg. 79

Mary H. Ross
SUNLIT POPPIES
28″ x 20″ O/C

Fred Grayson Sayre
OCOTILLOS IN BLOOM
8″ x 10″ O/C

Fred Grayson Sayre
THE SONG OF THE DESERT
40″ x 50″ O/C

Donna Norine Schuster
IN THE GARDEN, 1917
30″ x 30″ O/C   Pg. 81

Donna Norine Schuster
BOY WITH RABBIT
26″ x 20″ O/C

Donna Norine Schuster
TIGER LILIES
30″ x 30″ O/C   Pg. 83

Jack Wilkinson Smith
THE TRAIL OF GERONIMO
20″ x 24″ O/B

Jack Wilkinson Smith
FOG VEILED COAST
40″ x 48″ O/C

John Christopher Smith
CAMBRIA, CALIFORNIA
24″ x 30″ O/C   Pg. 85

John Christopher Smith
PLAZA
26″ x 34″ O/C

John Christopher Smith
HARBOR, SAN PEDRO
13″ x 16″ O/B

John Christopher Smith
HARVEST TIME
34″ x 50″ O/C

John Christopher Smith
MT. MAJESTIC, ZION CANYON
30″ x 40″ O/C   Pg. 86

John Christopher Smith
EARLY MORNING
24″ x 30″ O/C

John Christopher Smith
IRIS
30″ x 40″ O/C   Pg. 87

George Gardner Symons
GRAND CANYON
47″ x 70.50″ O/C   Pg. 89

George Gardner Symons
IRVINE COVE, LAGUNA BEACH
25″ x 30″ O/C

George Gardner Symons
CONNECTICUT SNOW SCENE
25″ x 30″ O/C   Pg. 90

George Gardner Symons
WINTER STREAM
25″ x 30″ O/C   Pg. 91
On loan from Paul & Kathleen Bagley

Stephen S. Thomas
THE BLIND MAN OF
PIERREFONDS
32″ x 25.50″ O/C

Christian von Schneidau
COLORFUL HILLS AT SUNSET
32″ x 40″ O/C

Christian von Schneidau
GIRL WITH NAUTILUS SHELL,
1920
30″ x 26″ O/C

Christian von Schneidau
PREENING
60″ x 45″ O/C   Pg. 93

Christian von Schneidau
FISH MARKET,
PROVINCETOWN
46″ x 56″ O/C   Pg. 94

Christian von Schneidau
POINSETTIAS
36″ x 30″ O/C   Pg. 95

Christian von Schneidau
THREE DRAWINGS: STUDIES
FOR FISH MARKET

Christian von Schneidau
LANDSCAPE WITH TWO GIRLS
17″ x 14″ O/C

Christian von Schneidau
THE SHADOWED HOUSETOPS
18″ x 24″ O/B

Elmer Wachtel
CALIFORNIA POPPIES
17″ x 24″ O/C   Pg. 97

Elmer Wachtel
CAPISTRANO MISSION
15″ x 25.50″ O/C   Pg. 99

Marion Kavanagh Wachtel
HIGH SIERRAS, CALIFORNIA
30″ x 40″ O/C

Marion Kavanagh Wachtel
LIFTING CLOUDS, OJAI
18″ x 24″ WC/P

Marion Kavanagh Wachtel
CHERRY VALLEY, CALIFORNIA
20″ x 26″ WC/P   Pg. 101
On loan from Paul & Kathleen Bagley

Abraham G. (Abel) Warshawsky
THE CLOWN
20″ x 16″ O/B

Abraham G. (Abel) Warshawsky
GIRL IN GREEN
32″ x 28″ O/C   Pg. 103

Abraham G. (Abel) Warshawsky
COTTAGE
9″ x 11.75″ O/B

William Wendt
HOME OF THE QUAIL, 1928
24″ x 32″ O/C   Pg. 105

William Wendt
SERENITY
30″ x 36″ O/C   Pg. 106
On loan from Paul & Kathleen Bagley

William Wendt
I LIFTED MINE EYES UNTO
THE HILLS
36″ x 50″ O/C   Pg. 107

111